HARDPRESS.NET

ISBN: 9781313396899

Published by:
HardPress Publishing
8345 NW 66TH ST #2561
MIAMI FL 33166-2626

Email: info@hardpress.net
Web: http://www.hardpress.net

BOBBINS OF BELGIUM

H.M. QUEEN ELISABETH OF BELGIUM

BOBBINS OF BELGIUM

A BOOK OF BELGIAN LACE, LACE-WORKERS, LACE-SCHOOLS AND LACE-VILLAGES

By

CHARLOTTE KELLOGG

Of the Commission for Relief in Belgium, and Author of "Women of Belgium"

FUNK & WAGNALLS COMPANY

NEW YORK AND LONDON

1920

Published in February, 1920

DEDICATION

To the women of the Brussels war-time lace committee—Madame Allard, the Vicomtesse de Beughem, Madame Kefer-Mali, and the Comtesse Elizabeth d'Oultremont, with admiration and gratitude.

CONTENTS

LIST OF ILLUSTRATIONS

PREFACE

PREFACE

I ENTERED the lace-world by the grim door of war. For it was the war-time work of the women of the Brussels Lace Committee that opened the way to me.

Long before the war, Queen Elizabeth in Belgium, like Queen Margharita in Italy, had sought means to protect the lace worker, through centuries the victim of an economic injustice, not to say crime, and to rescue and develop an industry threatened from many sides. In 1911 she gave her royal encouragement to a group of prominent Belgian women who organized as "Amies de la Dentelle," Friends of Lace, and began a lace-saving campaign by trying to remedy the deplorable condition of most of the lace schools, the defective teaching, long hours, and pitiful pay. They could insist in the schools, as they could not elsewhere, on the right to inspect, to grant or refuse patronage. They subsidized worthy institutions, and advocated the establishment of a lace normal school and of a special school of design. Education they felt to be the main road leading out of the prevailing misery, and they were making progress along this road, when suddenly the Invader poured over their borders.

While other women hurried to open refuges and hospitals and soup-kitchens, a few of the Friends of Lace remembered first the lace-makers; and by November 1914, had effected a war emergency organization, known as the Brussels Lace Committee, with Mrs. Whitlock as honorary president. Unfortunately most of the lace dealers failed to cooperate with them, but they won the approval of the powerful Belgian Comité National, which, with the Commission for Relief in Belgium, carried on the relief of the occupied territory throughout the war. And with an initial gift of $25,000 from America to be converted into lace, they were able to start their work. It soon came to be directed altogether by four women; The Comtesse Elizabeth d'Oultremont, Lady-in-Waiting to Queen Elizabeth; the Vicomtesse de Beughem, an American; Madame Josse Allard, and Madame Kefer-Mali. At the same time the aid and protection of workers on filets and other commonly called "imitation" laces, was assigned by the Comité National to another group of women, the "Union Patriotique des Femmes Belges."

The Brussels Lace Committee employed, as trusted business director of their offices, M. Collart, generously released to them by the Allard Bank, and as technical expert, Madame Sharlaecken, before the war with the Compagnie des Indes, one of the largest lace houses in

Belgium; and as the work developed, an increasing number of designers and aides necessary to a lace business were added.

During the first few months the situation seemed utterly hopeless; thread was impossible to obtain; and even if the thread were forthcoming, no one could say who would buy the laces they might encourage the women to make; the Germans were cutting off successive sections of the lace-making areas where they had established sub-committees, and were forbidding communication with them. And yet these four women continued bravely to create the foundations of a great lace business—for an extraordinary commercial organization grew from their efforts.

However, despite all their intelligence and devotion, such a result would have been impossible but for a hard-won diplomatic victory. In early 1915 Mr. Hoover forced an international agreement which permitted the C. R. B. to bring thread for the Lace Committee into Belgium, and to take out an equivalent weight in lace, to be sold in the Allied countries for the benefit of the workers. England required a rigid control of the thread, and that it be given only to establishments open to inspection by the C. R. B. At one time these thread shipments were stopt—a period of cruel anxiety for the women—but happily after a re-adjustment they were continued. And once these international guaranties were obtained, the Belgian Comité National was able to arrange for the distribution of the thread to the various, even remote, lace centers, and for the return of the finished laces to Brussels. They granted the women a subsidy of $10,000 and insured to each *dentellière* the chance to make at least three francs worth of lace a week—a small minimum, to be sure, but every one understood it might be increased later, and that if each of the many thousands of workers was to have an equal opportunity, it could not in the beginning be more. After this the Lace Committee had at times as many as 45,000 women on its lists. The work in the schools and out of them began to bear fruit. The sweating system, and payment in kind (in clothing and food) were practically wiped out, and inspection and control established. Everywhere the standard of design and of execution was raised; old patterns were restored and improved, and by the end of the war 2,237 new designs had been added.

But this was not advance through open country. There was constant danger that at any moment the way might be completely barred; at any time the guaranties covering the thread importations might be withdrawn. The Germans early originated a "Lace Control" of their own, and tried in every possible way to win over the Belgian workers, and to buy up all the lace in the country. They accused the Brussels Committee of being a political and patriotic body existing chiefly to defeat the occupying powers and the Flemish activists. Then there were other courage-testing difficulties. But despite all obstacles and perils, the women persisted, and continually the precious skeins of thread, with their message of "Carry On" were flung out from Brussels to the farthermost corners of the land, binding all together in a firm and beautiful web of hope and confidence. For the enemy was right in suspecting the Committee of a purpose deeper than that of merely trying to save women from the soup-line; they carried on a patriotic work of highest importance. To them I owe a personal debt of gratitude, for they permitted me to follow their devoted service closely, and they opened the door for me to a new world of beauty and interest.

INTRODUCTION

INTRODUCTION

LACE is a tissue composed of mesh and "flowers" (pattern), or either one alone, produced with a needle and single thread, or with several threads manipulated by means of bobbins. It is the product of a natural evolution from early embroideries and weaving.

We possess no contemporaneous history of the origins and development of the lace art, partly, perhaps, because of the tradition, strong among the initiated, of hiding its secrets, and of the consequent difficulty of an outsider to master them, and partly because successive wars and world cataclysms have interrupted or destroyed its progress.

We have ample proof, however, that

lace in some form existed in remote antiquity,—in early Egypt, in Persia, in Bysance and Syria, where it was chiefly made by slaves; the Greeks and Hebrews speak of needle lace as known throughout all time. It was not, in these oriental countries, the delicate white mesh that we call lace, which would have been most unbecoming to dark skin, but included richly colored passementeries and filets and fringes, woven of gold and silver thread, of dyed wool and cotton, and of the coarse linen fiber of the Nile Valley. It was usually of hieratic and symbolic design, and sometimes sown with gems—all capable of brilliantly enhancing the beauty of the East. Egyptian ladies of 6,000 years ago trimmed their robes with elaborate lengths of filet, and covered their dead with it. In the Cinquantenaire Museum at Brussels there is the photograph of a remarkable little woven linen bag, similar to one we might carry to-day, which was found in the tomb of a Priestess of Hathor, bearing the mark of one of the earlier dynasties. Its mesh is almost identical with that of our modern Valenciennes, and it was undoubtedly made with bobbins.

Between ancient and medieval times, the lace-gap is unbridged by written record; we must gather what we can from the archeologist and from the works of the sculptor and painter. Occasionally we are thrilled by such a discovery as that of M. Bixio, who in excavating at Claterna, an old Roman City near Bologna, came upon a set of bone bobbins, lying in pairs, as we employ them in lace-making to-day. But interesting discoveries are rare, and the body of our knowledge of lace history so far is meager.

However, we are interested primarily, not in the ancient origins of the two great lace groups, nor in early passementeries and filets and their processes, but in the marvelous efflorescence of the lace art of the Western Europe of the 16th, 17th and 18th centuries, and in its still lovely expression of to-day.

In medieval painting, before the appearance of linen and its use as trimming, or as lingerie, I know of no picture showing lace. Stuffs were stiff and heavy, and ornamented with metal, or with gold or silver thread. As they became more supple, we find, as in the portrait of Wenceslas of Luxemburg (about 1360) decoration introduced in the clipped cloth border of the collar and hood. This serrated edge suggests the first simple Cluny lace patterns that appeared later. Then we see the first linen showing through the slashed sleeve or above the corsage, —one of many paintings illustrating this development, is that of the Duke of Cleves, by Memling (second half of the 15th century). And shortly afterward the first lace edgings appear, the beginning of our lace of the middle ages, of its rebirth in Western Europe. The search for these details of progress in the paintings of European galleries is a fascinating and rewarding game; a Belgian friend of mine has spent many years at it.

The flowering of the lace-art was part of the great Renaissance (lagging behind, to be sure, the major arts) and now was no longer the work of slaves, but regarded as an important, independent *métier*, and happily it usually escaped the despotism of the medieval corporations. Italy, probably through her exploitation in the early part of the 15th century of her Greek Colonies, was its first western home, and Venice, the center for the exquisite needle laces of which our museums fortunately still preserve specimens. While laces made with the needle and single thread were flourishing under the Doges, bobbin laces, twisted and braided with many threads, were being made in Sicily and in other sections of the country.

From Venice, the secrets of the art traveled easily in several directions, and probably about the close of the 15th century by way of the thriving port of Antwerp, to the industrious and beauty-loving Flanders, where the seed fell on most fertile soil. Flanders possest a multitude of workers already skilled in an allied art, that of weaving, and the necessary lace material in her valley of the Lys, the finest flax region of the world. Valenciennes, Lille, Malines, Ghent, Bruges, turned to lace-making with a veritable passion; it spread throughout wide districts of what are now Northern France and Belgium.

During the 16th and 17th centuries, the lace industry made phenomenal progress, both extensively and intensively. Holland and England sent continually larger orders to Flanders. As cloths grew finer and softer, and the mode of wearing them more graceful, and as daintier linens were increasingly employed, lace became ever more filmy and exquisite. A worker spent perhaps a whole year on a single meter of Valenciennes, one head-dress cost as much as 200,000 livres. Every lace had its time, its season. During this epoch, needle laces were supreme, as bobbin laces were to be in the 18th century.

Under Louis XIV lace reached its climax of perfection and beauty. Colbert imported lace-women from each center where they had been conspicuously successful. He encouraged the invention of new designs and technique; he subsidized schools in many cities, at Reims, Alençon, Arras, Sedan, and he threatened with the death penalty those who might attempt to carry lace secrets beyond the French borders,—in every way he sought to develop an art that should belong peculiarly to France. Thus directed and subsidized by the state, and nurtured and stimulated by a beauty-seeking court, whose love of luxury was still controlled by taste and refinement, it is not surprizing that this lace-period surpassed any other known. It was true of the Court of Louis XIV as of that of Louis XIII that a *seigneur* was known by the number and quality of his lace points; some of them possest several hundred garnitures. Unfortunately the workers did not profit by this brilliant development,—they seem from the beginning predestined to be the victims of a social and economic slavery.

But there were already evidences of an attempt to control a demand for luxury that threatened disaster. With the 16th century, heavy duties and excess taxes were levied upon lace. An edict, dated 1729, prohibited the wearing of it, in the hope of checking over-extravagance in dress.

After its *apogée* under Louis XIV, lace-making was caught, along with the other arts, in the tide of degeneracy. Its designs were marked by fantasy and grotesqueness, rather than by the delicacy and beauty of the preceding period; tho while it deteriorated in design, its technique grew constantly finer and more complicated, until, from the point of view of the workmanship at least, it seemed almost superhuman. But in the second half of the 18th century, wearied of complications and extravagance, people amused themselves by a return to simplicity. The Marquise de Pompadour affected laces sown with simple "flowers," and Marie Antoinette went further in preferring a pattern of scattered "points" or peas. With this return to the primitive in design, the technique of lace reverted also. In many quarters, the sheer muslins of the Indias gained favor over lace. Trade, already burdened with the duties and imports that had grown up around the extravagant laces, suffered further from the sudden popularity of the simple costume.

The death-blow of the industry in France was to follow close on the heels of this new fashion. Since lace had been the particular pride of the aristocrat, the Revolution made it a crime to appear in it. In such one-time famous centers as Valenciennes and Lille, the bobbins ceased, tho the industry of that region sought refuge farther west, in Bailleul,—in Bailleul, dust and ashes to-day! Fortunately in Belgium, lace-making generally survived the crisis of the Revolution, tho it has suffered from succeeding disastrous influences.

At the opening of the 19th century and under the Empire, taste was heavy, design rigid and military, with nothing in common with true lace motifs. During the opening years of 1800 the invention of machine-made tulle, brought from England to Calais, effected further sad changes in the lace-world; scarfs, veils, entire robes of tulle, ornamented with applications of needle or bobbin-made details—often palms and laurel wreaths—were all the mode. People preferred these to the exquisite lace jabots and flounces of the preceding century. In 1833 cotton thread began to be used instead of the stronger linen of the best lace periods. The delicate lace-art continued to suffer with all the others under the general decadence of the reign of Louis Philippe and the Second Empire. Industrial and commercial development was the note of the age; the rich amused themselves in travel, in new scenes and sports, rather than in fostering the arts. In fact, during the thirty years following the war of 1870, lace seemed almost forgotten except in America. The number of workers in Belgium fell from between 100 and 150,000, to 50,000 or less.

But before the world was plunged into this last, most destructive of wars, there had been signs of a renaissance in the decorative arts. People had begun to read and compare, and refine their taste. The rulers of Italy and France and Belgium were winning results in their attempts to rescue, and to revive and develop the lace-art, which had seemed threatened with extinction. Then came the war—and the devastation of entire lace regions, like that of Bailleul in France, and of Ypres in Belgium. It is true that many of the refugee lace-women have been employed and encouraged during the four years, by certain committees in France and free Belgium. And in occupied Belgium, the unceasing efforts of the Brussels Lace Committee have borne rich fruit. Whether the higher standards of lace design and technique, and the improved condition of the lace workers—better education, shorter hours, higher pay—will be maintained under post-war conditions is yet to be proved. Over this difficult hour of reconstruction, of transfer from war to what we fondly call normal conditions, we can but hope to carry the hard-won gains of the testing period.

In this little book I make no attempt to present a history of lace, or a detailed analysis of its processes. I have wished merely to set down in simple form a few of my observations in the lace districts of Belgium, as the war has left her. To follow them one does not need even an elementary knowledge of the important lace forms, tho that is easily acquired. For there are but two large groups; the needle-lace group, and the bobbin-lace group, between which we learn quickly to distinguish. We can not prove the time of their respective origins; as we know them, they seem to have existed side by side, as they do in the Belgium of to-day. Sometimes one was more popular, sometimes the other.

To place a piece of lace, we have first but to ask the question, "Was it made with a needle, and by looping and twisting and weaving a single thread; or was it made by braiding and twisting and weaving several threads, by means of bobbins and a round or a square cushion?"

In general, there is but one technique for all needle laces, tho there is no limit to the variety of stitches the needle worker may employ. I have seen a scarf, made during the war for Queen Elizabeth, in which there were many hundred different points. One comes soon to recognize the important needle laces; the exquisite French Alençons and Argentins of earlier days, with their meshes made with a button-hole loop, and their flowers stiffened with horsehair; the various Venetian points,—Venise, Burano, and Rose point; and the extremely popular Brussels point, with its gauze mesh and raised flowers. It is characteristic of these needle laces, that the flowers are thrown into relief, sometimes high, sometimes scarcely perceptible.

Bobbin laces may be made with a dozen or with one hundred times as many threads, according to the design and width of the lace. They fall into two sub-groups, the first including laces made with uncut threads, in a single piece; the second, those made detail by detail, in which the threads are cut as each is finished, the completed lace piece being made by joining these separate parts. This second method was not introduced until the latter half of the 17th century.

In the first group, made with uncut threads, are the early Clunys and the common Torchons, Old Flanders, the beautiful Valenciennes, Point de Paris, Point de Lille, Malines and Binche, with their delicate round, or square or hexagonal meshes, from which the pattern blossoms. Their flowers are flat, never lifted in relief, tho a heavy outlining thread often sets them off brilliantly from the surrounding field.

The second bobbin group, in which the final lace piece is composed of united details, includes black and white Chantilly, Blonde, popular with Spanish peoples, Brussels Duchesse and Bruges Duchesse, most frequently displayed in our American shops, and the finer Rosaline, which was in great demand when the war broke out. This group of bobbin laces admits a kind of relief.

Some laces combine both needle and bobbin points. In the lovely Point d'Angleterre, increasingly difficult to obtain, bobbin-made flowers are united by an

PORTRAIT TOWARD CLOSE OF SIXTEENTH CENTURY
Showing collar ornamented with bobbin-made cluny

ANNE OF AUSTRIA BY VAN DYCK
About 1635, cluny lace made with bobbins

airy needle mesh. And the coarser Flanders lace has the same composition.

There are, besides, the familiar and often beautiful Applications, in which either needle or bobbin-made flowers are stitched, or *appliquéd* on machine-made tulle, or, rarely, on a tulle made by hand. And various mixed laces, fantasies and embroidered tulles, as well as a whole company of cheaper tissues called lace, but which can not honestly claim the name, are trying always to crowd the true lace from the market.

Naturally, the technique of any given kind of lace has undergone various transformations through the centuries. The Valenciennes mesh, for instance, first had round spaces, while square ones became more popular later. During a certain period the introduction of jours, or openwork effects, added an airy lightness to many laces.

I had the pleasure recently of being

with a friend of mine, the sister of the Belgian Consul-General at New York, Madame Kefer-Mali, who has devoted twenty years to the study of lace, when she first examined a lace collection lately presented to the Cinquantenaire Museum. With magnifying glass I followed from case to case, as she placed each specimen in its country and century, according to its design, its mesh, the manner of directing the threads, the relief of the flowers, the various stitches or the kind of thread employed. As I listened to her, it was easy to appreciate why lace may become an all-absorbing interest. Madame Kefer-Mali's love for the lace itself is now subordinate to her passionate desire to secure justice for the lace-worker. As she takes a filmy length in her hand, her first thought is of the talent and patience of the girl or woman who made it, of the eye-straining, meticulous labor it represents, and of the pittance still paid her for her gift to the world of art. Madame Kefer-Mali has already won something for the *dentellière* and she will continue to fight for more.

Tho there are lace sections in widely scattered parts of Belgium, none (except Turnhout) is so important as those of the two Flanders. Western and Eastern Flanders form an almost continuous and unrivalled lace region, which breaks up irregularly into districts, each celebrated for a particular kind, or for several kinds of lace. However, it would be impossible to draw an accurate map illustrating the Belgian lace situation, either from the point of view of the varieties made and their quality, or of the workers. It seems, indeed, at times that lace was invented to defeat the statistician, for he no sooner reaches a conclusion than it proves inexact; a factory rises near a certain river and the lace women desert their cushions to accept its better wages; in a village long devoted to Needle Point, young girls discover that the bobbin-made Clunys pay better, or they marry and make no lace at all until their children are partly grown; poor crops and resulting misery may send others who have not for some time been listed as workers back to their cushions. For, since despite the many schools and work-rooms, the great majority of women still work at home, lace-making is peculiarly sensitive to every change in family and community life. We may say, however, that despite constantly shifting conditions, Western Flanders forms a great bobbin-lace area, unquestionably the most important in the world to-day, while Eastern Flanders has been for centuries and still is, famous for its needle points.

Unfortunately, too, because of the miserable lace-wage (in Belgium, before the war, it averaged about a franc a day) this industry has been regarded always as a supplementary occupation, on which the family could not rely for its main support, and which was not capable of organization and amelioration as other industries are. The slavery conditions have undoubtedly been due chiefly to lack of good schools and constructive lace training, and to the system by which a *facteur,* or first buyer, collects the laces, to re-sell them to a *fabricant,* or dealer, who in turn may sell them to a larger fabricant—a system permitting any number of intermediaries—and also to the fact that the women, scattered as they are throughout the agricultural regions, have never protected themselves by forming syndicates. The first step toward emancipation has been taken; the new teaching is under way. The fatal system of the many intermediaries remains to be dealt with—to be swept away. And it is hoped that feeling the new power education will give them, the dentellières will at last find ways either through unions or by other means, of protecting themselves.

For the rest, fixt data are difficult to obtain. The lace industry can not be captured and subjected to cold analysis and tabulation. It must be studied differently from other industries that can be localized. As in learning to know the garden flowers of a country, one must go from doorstep to doorstep, so if one wishes to understand lace, one should become familiar with its *milieu,* the family and community life from which it springs. In a sense, then, these little journeys to lace districts which are the subjects of my chapters, may suggest more about what lace really is than a more technical and formidable volume.

I

TURNHOUT

FIFTEENTH CENTURY PORTRAIT
Showing heavy brocade as yet unrelieved by linen or lace trimming

PORTRAIT OF CHARLES IX (1570)
Linen collar showing picot edge made with the needle

WEDDING GIFT OF MR. HOOVER TO MRS. PAGE

Executed in Venise and Flanders lace by 30 women working three months. American eagles with outspread wings, protecting the Belgian Lion enchained in the four corners

FLANDERS—NEEDLE MESH, BOBBIN FLOWERS

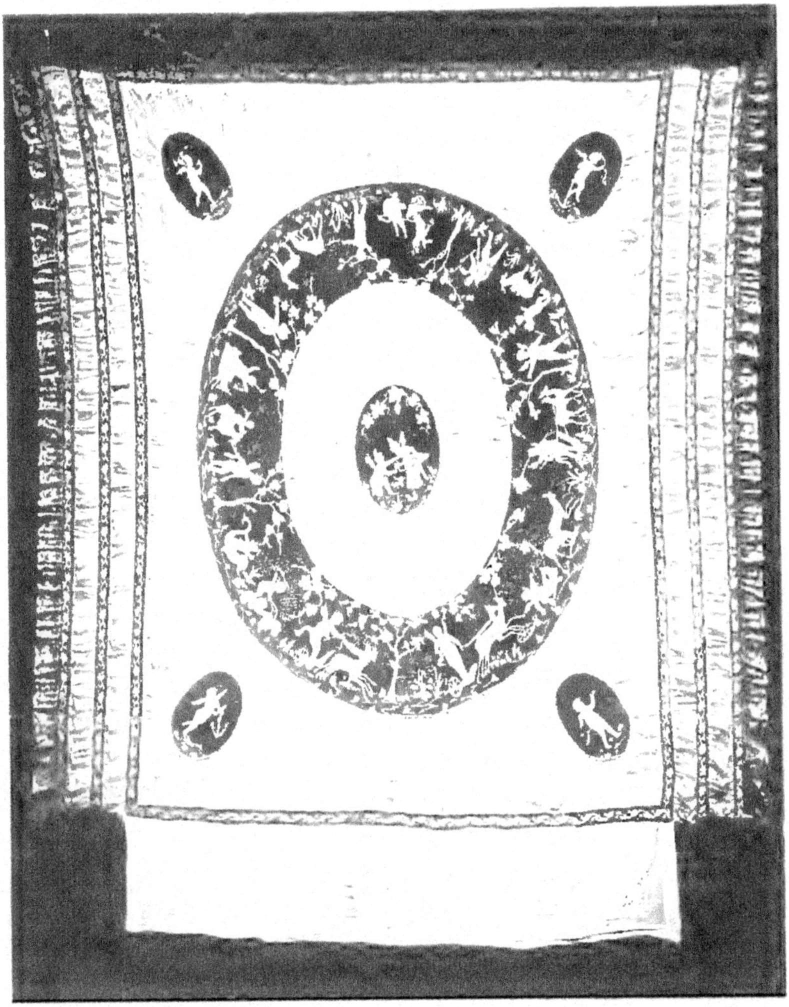

VENISE LACE CENTER, BORDER OF VALENCIENNES

Lace executed in Flanders by 40 women in two months; embroidery and mounting in Brussels by four women in three months

VALENCIENNES, SQUARE MESH

I

TURNHOUT

Lace Children of the North

LACE is the flower of Belgium; the white blossom that springs from the teeming plains of the Flanders, from the agricultural districts, and from the mournful Campine of the North. During the long and solitary winters, when work in the fields is impossible, thousands of women and girls and little children turn to their lace cushions, and dreary rooms are enlivened by the music of the flying bobbins. If the lace is Needle Point, and lacks the accompanying click-clack of the shifting *fuseaux,* it nevertheless gives purpose and value to the otherwise almost unsupportable winter days. However, despite the time that must be subtracted for weeding, for gathering the all-important potato crop, and for other farm duties, summer with its bright light and long day, is the true lace season; it is only then that some of the finest varieties can be executed. Coarser pieces must be substituted for the dull, eye-straining days.

To be sure, some lace-making is still carried on in certain cities, but very little. This delicate *métier* can not successfully combat the influences of the social and industrial groupings of the larger centers; the living wage, the shorter hours, the distractions of cinéma and café. The cities remain the logical centers for the normal and training-schools, for assembling, and display, and sale; but the age-old patience of the lace-maker is born of a certain ignorance and isolation. This does not mean that the industry may not persist still on the fringes of some of the larger cities, or flourish in nearby villages—it does; and in three conspicuous instances, until the war, it remained the dominating activity of a city. Bruges, Ypres, and Turnhout, could truly be called "lace cities." Now there are but two; for Ypres, the pearl of Flanders, is gone.

Turnhout, a town of 24,000 inhabitants, in the Northern Campine district, is not only a "lace city," counting 6,000 workers, but if one considers its long list of excellent lace-schools, the fine varieties made there, and the quality of the workmanship, it appears sufficiently important to challenge the leadership of Bruges. However, Turnhout stands practically alone in the north, while Bruges is the center of western Flanders, one of the largest lace contributing areas in Belgium, and promises, therefore, to hold for a long time her title of first lace-city.

It is strange to think of Turnhout as

a remote town, since it is scarcely two hours by motor from Antwerp; but the first glimpse of the intervening sand wastes of the Campine region awakens at once a sensation of loneliness, of isolation. I made the journey in late November, reaching Turnhout about noon of a low gray day, just as hundreds of golden-haired children—no mists could dull the bright gold of their hair—were clattering along the stone sidewalks in their wooden shoes, on their way home from school. As always, I marveled at the way they could leap and run without losing their sabots. They were "lace children," nearly all of them part of the little army of 1,800 in the lace-schools, and because of the intelligent work of the soup-kitchens and dining-rooms for debilitated children during the four years of war, were probably, many of them, in better physical condition than they had been at its beginning. The women of the

Brussels Lace Committee had succeeded, too, in augmenting their food ration from time to time. Their chief visible need was for stockings and shoes—and I knew from the teachers later that they sadly lacked underclothes. Mothers can patch and repatch, and add in various ways to outer garments; but after a certain number of washings, undergarments simply disappear.

I went first to the convent of the Abbé Berraly which, during the war, encouraged by the advice and support of the Lace Committee, has developed into the model school of Belgium. It is situated in a crowded part of the town, but its own fine brick buildings cluster about a spacious courtyard and vegetable gardens. In summer the children work much out of doors, tho when they are inside their class-rooms it seems still impossible for the teachers to break with the tradition of the closed window.

I began my visit in a little room at the right of the entrance hall, where six older girls were still at work, tho the 500 other pupils had gone for their lunch. Dozens of rubbed carbon copies of lace patterns were pinned to the walls along with executed samples of the lace they represented. This was a *piqué* class-room; the young women seated at high, narrow tables, were carefully at work on pieces of glossy green cardboard on which the lace design had been drawn and which they were pricking with pins, or covering with tiny holes, that indicate the position of the pins that must hold the thread as it is twisted or looped or braided. by the worker. The cardboard piqué is in a sense both the beginning and the end of the lace course; the beginning, since no pupil can start his lace without the piqué, or interpreted pattern, and the end, since it is the most difficult of all the processes in the technique of the lace. The *piqueuse* must understand the design and its practical execution, must interpret the picture to the worker in terms of pin-pricks marking the progress of her thread. A good piqueuse knows immediately, on looking at a drawing, whether it is a true lace design, or must be adapted, and also in which kind of lace it can be best exprest. As she shifts a pin-prick less than a hair's width to the left or to the right she varies appreciably the resulting mesh or flower. She has considerable liberty in deciding which particular stitches will be most effective to fill in the jours, or open-work spaces indicated in the pattern.

One of the great evils of the past has been the absence of training-schools, and the consequent lack of piqueuses; in each generation there have been but a few good ones, who have, in a sense, held the lace industry in their hands. Before the war, Ypres had two famous piqueuses, to whom patterns were sent from an entire region; and in the town of Turnhout to-day, with its thousands of workers, tho there are several less experienced piqueuses, there is but one woman to whom the finest and most complicated drawings can be entrusted for interpretation. She is the only person, for example, who could make the piqué for the beautiful scarf, which I saw later being executed in the Point de Paris room—for that she received 90 francs. It is a common saying that one must be born a piqueuse to succeed; at least it remains true that in addition to her capacity for an intricate and most meticulous labor, the piqueuse should possess a high sensitiveness to art values.

The little room in the Abbé Berraly's school is one expression of the Lace Committee's conviction that the emancipation of the industry and of the lacemaker will come only through education.

ABBÉ BERRALY SCHOOL, TURNHOUT
General view

NINE-YEAR-OLD CHILDREN MAKING POINT DE PARIS

in general the women of the past have sat dumbly before their cushions, helpless to do anything but continue to execute, year after year, the particular cardboard pattern the facteur, or lace agent, placed before them. They had little or no conception of the rich art world of which their flowered flounces were a part, and no feeling at all of their power to influence that world by interpreting a design for themselves, or by correcting or improving it, or even perhaps by creating a new one. Not that all workers should become designers, or even piqueuses—progress depends, as it does in other industries, on specialization; but at least trained workers will enjoy the freedom to choose and the feeling of independence that comes from a thorough knowledge of their *métier*.

In this room then was a class of specialists, six smiling, intelligent young women between 16 and 18 equipping themselves as experts in interpretation. The designs on which they worked, many of them revivals of classic ones long forgotten, or beautiful recent creations of Belgian artists, had been sent up to them from the Committee's central room of design in Brussels. Before the war, they would have come from the particular lace dealer to whose agent their laces were sold.

Opening from the little pattern room I found the office with its great oak armoire, where the costly finished laces are stored until the day they are taken to Brussels, to be combined into beautiful confections for the salon or bedroom or dining-room, or for personal adornment. Of course, some are always resold by the meter, but one of the chief successes of the Lace Committee has been the employment of motifs and yard laces in the production of cloths and spreads and innumerable articles of a loveliness hitherto unknown.

From the office and the little room where the pricked cardboard patterns are prepared for the cushions, I went further along the hall, and turned to the left, where at the foot of a staircase were new wooden benches awaiting the sabots of the returning children. These benches were new because the Germans, who, here as elsewhere, had driven the children from their school, had burned their benches, and not only the benches, but all visible wood—they had torn casements from the windows and doorways, as well as removing every knob and fixture. This was disgusting, but more or less understandable. Their country demanded more cannon, therefore they took brass and copper; they were cold, so they ripped off the nearest available piece of wood. But wood and metal failed to satisfy them; upstairs at one end of the largest room there is a pretty stage arranged for school festivals, with a painted forest background, and side wing-drops picturing meadow-lands. These fathers and brothers of German children slashed and ripped the painted canvas forest and ran their bayonets through the foreground meadows, with no spur beyond that of the pleasure in the act; for no inch of the canvas had been taken away—I could have replaced the whole from the rags.

It was still only a little past one o'clock, and the children had not yet returned. I went into the beginners' room, where large windows let in all the light there was on this gray day, and saw the long, even rows of low rush-seated, high-backed chairs, with the school-room sabots (where the children were fortunate enough to possess this second pair) hanging from the backs. Before each chair was a round or square work-cushion and over each cushion a white cloth carefully spread to protect the precious thread-bearing bobbins beneath. The whole empty, silent place seemed prepared for a ceremonial or religious rite; and every snowy cushion a tiny altar awaiting its ministrant.

At last they were coming back, the younger children clattering in ahead of the older girls, to deposit their muddy street sabots on the benches. Such a rush of yellow-haired babies for their chairs—several of them were no more than seven years old; many were between nine and ten. Little feet slipt into the clean sabots, white cloths were carefully lifted and folded, sisters and teachers began their rounds of inspection and instruction, as tiny hands took their positions over the heaps of bobbins—one at the left, one at the right—and the cadence of the clicking wood began. It was impossible for me to follow these incredible little fingers as they twisted and braided from pin to pin. I had seen scales so rapidly played that the successive motions were only a blur, but these shiftings back and forth of the bobbins were even more bewildering. More strangely moving than the picture of any great orchestra where gifted fingers wrung melody from a myriad of strings, was this of the play of hundreds of baby hands over threads and bobbins, as the flowers blossomed beneath them. It is said that to become a good lace-maker one must begin, as he would if he expected to become a distinguished pianist, at latest at the age of seven or eight.

The greater number of these little girls were making Point de Paris edgings. They had their pricked patterns pinned near the top of the square linen-covered cushions and were working the threads vertically toward them. Since the pins which hold the threads in place must be constantly moved along as the work proceeds, it is very important that the cushion should be stuffed with something that the pins can easily penetrate. These particular cushions were stuffed with wool, some contain straw, and the linen covering was blue, tho it is often the natural color. Besides guiding the tiny brass pins (which vary with the delicacy of the lace) that hold the thread, each child must know how to manipulate the long brass pins which separate the various groups of bobbins not in actual use. She learns, too, to roll each finished section of her lace in blue paper and tuck it carefully away in the little drawer below the upper part of the cushion; the true lace-maker prides herself on the snowy whiteness of her lace, which she protects in every conceivable way.

While I was moving from one to another, a sister had gathered a group of seven to ten year olds nearer the stove—

a company of Fra Angelico angels they looked, as I bent over them to watch their little hands. They placed brass pins in the holes pricked in the pattern to hold the rather coarse thread, twisted first two threads to the right, then two to the left, then braided them to form the familiar hexagon of the Point de Paris mesh. When they reached the pattern, a most simple conventional one, other bobbins had to be brought into play. They held the threads always from the top of the cushion vertically toward them, with the seam edge of the lace to the left and the border to the right. Even these babies had from 50 to 200 bobbins to keep in mind, rather long beech-wood bobbins, these for Point de Paris, with the thread tightly wound at the top, and a considerable pear-shaped bulge at the end. Each lace is supposed to require a particular bobbin, especially suited to the weight of thread employed, but workers

POINT DE PARIS CLASS

On dark days lamps are lighted behind bottles filled with water, the rays passing through fall in spotlights on the cushions

WINDING BOBBINS FOR THE CHILDREN

often use them indifferently. Some fortunate ones pride themselves on their fine ebony or ivory sets. Of course, bobbins must be constantly resupplied with thread, and in a corner of the room I saw a white-haired grandmother with her *dévidoir,* or spindle, busily winding thread on the bobbins for the children. She made a beautiful picture there at her wheel with a dozen little girls with their cushions crowding near her. I asked if the beginners were able to earn something and found they were making about 10 and 15 cents a day.

In this model school, for all children under sixteen years of age the lace work alternates with regular lessons, as it should of course, in every school. Those above that age may give their entire day to the lace. The hours for girls between nine and thirteen are: from 8 to 11 o'clock, lessons; from 1:30 to 4 o'clock, lessons again; and from 4 to 6:30 o'clock, lace.

This is still a sadly long day for growing children, but it nevertheless registers a most cheering improvement over the former cruelty of a far longer day. It has been the Committee's hope that such a system as this might be instituted throughout Belgium, and that from it they might advance to still better conditions. Children from thirteen to sixteen come at 7:30 o'clock, make lace till 11:30, and again from 1:30 to 4:45 o'clock. From 5 until 6:30 o'clock they have regular school lessons—one wonders how much education can be crowded into one and a half hours at the end of a day that began at 7:30 o'clock! The girls over sixteen years of age make lace from 7:30 until 6:30 o'clock. One thing to remember always, in looking at these distressing figures, is the frequent number of holidays in Belgium; the children are saved by their numerous *fête* days.

It was not easy to leave the tragic

and marvelous primary room; the fairy-like fingers and the golden heads above the cushions. But I had to go on to room number one on the ground floor where there was another Point de Paris class, for girls about twelve years old. In the Abbé Berraly school the girls must pass through at least three classes in Point de Paris before they proceed to Point de Lille, to go on from there to the "spider-web," or delicate and most difficult Malines.

The first striking difference between this room and the primary, was in the number of bobbins piled on the cushions —there were hundreds now instead of dozens. The cushions were larger, too, and most of them were round, for many of the pupils were working on collars and doily and handkerchief edgings. The designs were already complicated, one of them represented, for instance, the animal symbols of the allied nations. This class promotes to the advanced class in Point de Paris, where I found several cushions with over 500 bobbins heaped upon them, and girls of fourteen and fifteen years shifting that number with a swiftness not to be followed.

Since the heavy rain was making seeing difficult, the teachers moved a number of iron stands (resembling umbrella stands) to various points in the room, placing on top of each stand, in the middle, a small kerosene lamp, and, near the edge, a large globular carafe, filled with water. The light from the lamp passes through the bottle to fall with concentrated and magnifying effect directly on that spot on the cushion where the work is in progress. The rack may be turned, the bottle raised or lowered, and usually four girls profit by the light from one lamp. It is a picturesque and primitive system, which many still prefer to the more modern and expensive electricity, because it is an advantage to have the working spot on the cushion thrown into high relief, while at the same time the bottle light is softer and less tiring to the eyes than electricity. These iron stands and lamps were very practical and satisfactory, but I have often seen, in poor little rooms, the bottle set on the table on a rough wooden block, with a rude oil dip in a cup propped up on bits of stick or stone behind it to lift it to just the proper height; as the work progresses, the position of course must be altered.

While the girls were pulling their chairs closer to the bottles I talked with the teachers about the place of Point de Paris in the lace world. There is no fine lace, they told me, which is so much in demand to-day as Point de Paris, for no lace so successfully combines durability and beauty. It is more used for dainty lingerie than any other variety. Paris buyers seem never to be able to secure sufficient Point de Paris, which tho it was christened by that city and was largely produced there during the 17th century, must now be supplied by Belgium. Its strength depends on its solid hexagonal mesh, always the test of lace, which is made with eight cotton threads, usually of fairly coarse quality. From this substantial mesh may blossom a pattern of extreme grace and beauty, the closely woven flat parts or toile, being relieved by open-work spaces, or jours, and the whole design outlined and thus thrown into a kind of relief by a heavier thread. The roses of the Queen design, drawn for the Brussels Committee by Mlle. Brouhon (who has since died), is one of the loveliest of the recent ones. I saw, the other day, a box scented with lavender and filled with rolls upon rolls of this rose pattern lace, ready for the day when a château can be restored, and fine linen sheets and pillow slips with their Point de Paris edgings can once again be spread on the beds.

Point de Lille could never be successfully used for either lingerie or table or bed linen for it is not sufficiently durable. In room 3, girls from fourteen to sixteen years were beginning to execute this more difficult lace. Its clear, transparent mesh originated in the city from which it is named, where in 1788 there were as many as 16,000 women employed on it. Its fragility results from the fact that but four threads (instead of the customary eight of Point de Paris and Malines, and of the mother of them all, Valenciennes) are used in twisting and braiding the meshes. On its light, clear mesh, the designs are now often very elegant and free, tho the traditional Point de Lille edging has a straight border and rather rigid pattern. They are always outlined by a heavier thread, as are the flowers of the Point de Paris and Malines, but unlike these other laces, the Point de Lille is characterized by little *pois,* or peas or dots, scattered through the mesh. It is sometimes confused with Malines because of the transparency of its mesh, which, however, is not so delicate as that of Malines, nor so difficult to make, nor, because of its fewer threads, so solid.

One of the most popular and more solid varieties of Point de Lille is better known as Point d'Hollande, because it is chiefly sold to the well-to-do Dutch peasants for their handsome bonnets. It is wide and often of sumptuous design, a sole branch or flower frequently furnishing the entire wing of a bonnet.

In the classroom, I went directly to a dark-haired Josephine, whose cushion seemed to hold the largest mounds of bobbins—"Yes, there are over a thousand," she admitted shyly and smilingly. The directress came to help her open the little drawer beneath her round cushion,

POINT DE LILLE, OR POINT D'HOLLANDE; MESH SHOWING "ESPRITS" OR DOTS CHARACTERISTIC OF THIS BOBBIN LACE

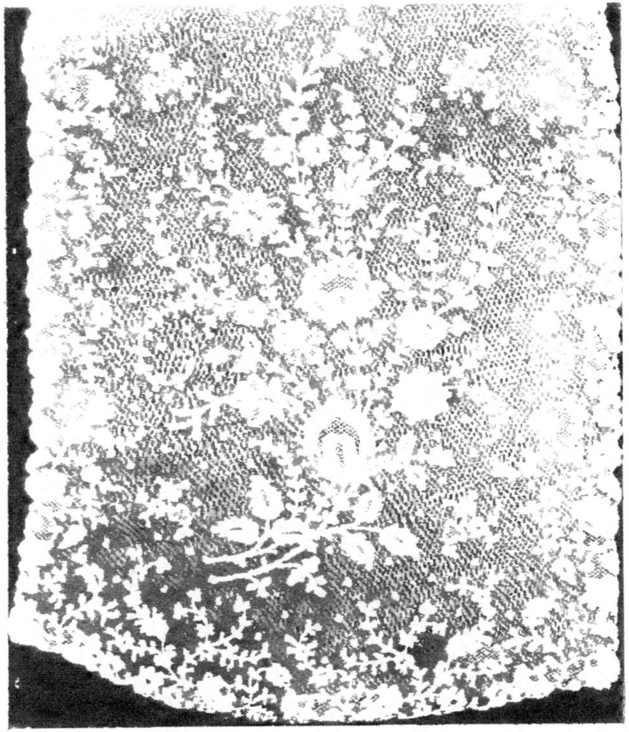

END OF A POINT DE PARIS SCARF ABOUT $2\frac{1}{2}$ YARDS LONG ON WHICH COLETTE WORKED ONE YEAR

IN THE ABBÉ BERRALY SCHOOL, COLETTE, 16 YEARS OLD, WORKS WITH 1,000 BOBBINS

and to shake from the blue paper a most lovely wide scarf with a charming flower design. "I began it last January," she added, "and I hope to finish it this January of 1919." One year with a thousand bobbins, and at best 50 cents a day for her work—which was so much more than she could have made before the war that she had no thought of complaining! I wondered if the woman who would throw this filmy flower-sown veil over her shoulders would care to know about the dark-eyed Josephine and her year with the 1,000 bobbins.

But there is much more beautiful lace than either Point de Paris or Point de Lille taught in the Turnhout school. The girls pass from the Lille room to Malines, known in the city of its birth as the "spider-web of Malines." Nothing could be more airy and exquisite than its delicate hexagonal mesh, much more difficult to make than either of the preceding varieties because it must be worked without the aid of pins, with only the eye to guide in securing the requisite uniformity and exactness. No lace demands greater skill or greater patience; since in addition to the difficulty of working without supporting pins, is the difficulty of handling the extremely fine thread employed. The patterns are usually of delicate flowers and leaves, with open-work stitches introduced to add ever greater lightness to the whole.

The dentellières in the Malines room work chiefly on insertions and flounces to be used for handkerchiefs or fichus or dainty blouses, or perhaps for wedding gowns. The Committee has given them, too, many orders for inserts for table centers or doilies, so exquisite that one feels they should be used only under glass.

Scarcely an important family in Belgium but treasures a bit of old Malines. Among my rarest pleasures were those I enjoyed, when the conversation turning upon lace, a friend has said: "But would you care to see my mother's Malines, or my great, great-grandmother's?"—and she has brought from a brocade box a filmy, ivory-colored collar or flounce, or a scarf or bonnet, all of a breath-taking loveliness and delicacy never to be reproduced. I remember, too, a Christmas mass and the marvelous flounce that fell from beneath the white and gold chasuble worn by Cardinal Mercier over the scarlet of his robe.

It is only in Turnhout that any considerable quantity of Malines is yet made, and despite all the efforts of the Committee and of other lovers of beautiful lace, there is little hope that it will live much longer. When the old artists, for so they should be named, die, few young women are found willing still to sacrifice their years to the spider-web.

The women of the Lace Committee

believe there is no future work more important than that of improving the 200 and more lace schools of their country. In the lace normal school at Bruges, in the national school of design at Brussels, the excellent Needle Point school at Zele, and in such schools as this one at Turnhout, they see the hope of the lace art; they urge that the Government increase its subsidies to these and other deserving institutions. Education and ever better education of the lace-woman is their watchword.

II

COURTRAI

II

COURTRAI

Early Home of Valenciennes

FOR years I had heard of the blue flax fields of the valley of the Lys, and of the season between April and September, when along miles of its course, the river is filled with boxes floating the finest linen fiber of the world, the flax of Belgium, North France and Holland, which can be better prepared in its waters than anywhere else.

Unfortunately I could see it only under a January rain, but Monsieur de Stoop, a prominent weaver of Courtrai, the town of 36,000 inhabitants which is the valley center, made the Flanders fields bloom again as he described to me the successive steps which lead from them to the woven linen his factory produces—I should say, produced, for the Germans left his plant, along with seven others, an utter ruin. He was unable to explain and apparently no analysis has yet determined, just why the waters of the Lys river surpass all others in their power to rot the encasing straw and generally to cleanse the flax; but one thing is clear, they have established Courtrai as a world market for fine raw linen. Sometimes the stalks need be floated only two or three days, sometimes it requires very much longer to macerate them, the period depending chiefly on the weather, and particularly on the temperature.

After its soaking and cleansing, the linen fiber starts again on its journey, this time to the various countries where it is to be made into thread and woven into tissues. Much goes to England and

BELGIAN LACE MESHES (Plate I)

After Pierre Verhagen in "La Dentelle Belge"

All meshes made with bobbins: 1 and 4, Valenciennes, round mesh; 2, Valenciennes, square mesh; 3, Valenciennes, mesh almost round; 5, Chantilly; 6, Old Flanders; 7, Point de Paris

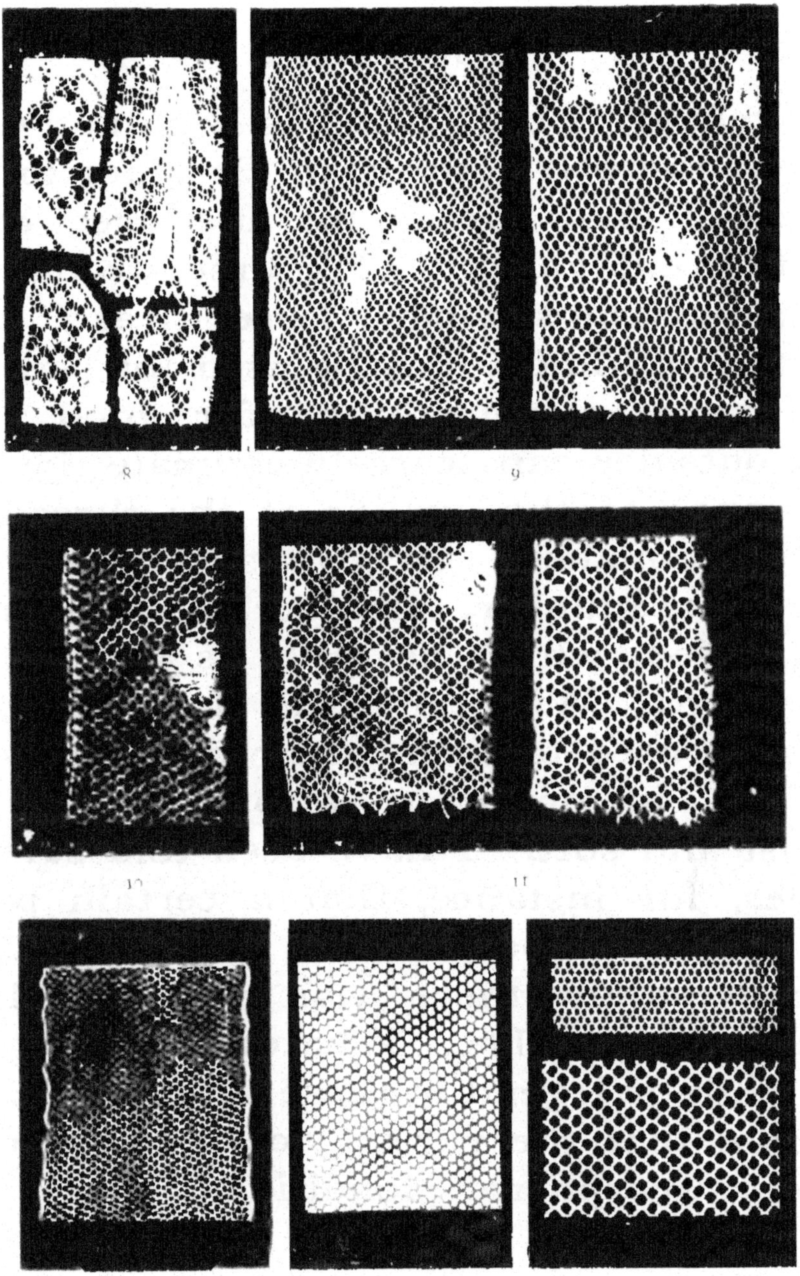

12 13 14

BELGIAN LACE MESHES (Plate II)

After Pierre Verhagen in "La Dentelle Belge"

Meshes, 8 to 12, made with bobbins: 8, Binche; 9, Malines; 10, Point de Lille, made for France; 11, Point de Lille, destined for Holland; 12, Gauze Point, made with needle, used in Point d'Angleterre; 13, Brussels machine-made net; 14, Ordinary machine-made net.

to Ireland, to such firms as Beth and Cox. From there it returns to Belgium in the form of linen thread for fine laces, quite a different variety, of course, from that employed in sewing. Lace thread, both cotton and linen, may be used for sewing, but never sewing-thread for good lace. An outsider can scarcely estimate the importance of the quality of the thread to the lace-maker. Of two skeins bearing the same number, one may be supple and easily led, while the other is brittle and wayward. We hear many stories of how women used to spend their lives in damp cellars, in order to keep their thread moist and soft. I have been told several times, for instance, that a certain piece of lace had been made below ground, because only there was its marvelous technique possible. Whatever the degree of truth or legend in these assertions, it is known that the rarest laces require certain atmospheric conditions, and are, above all, dependent on a superior fineness and pliability of the thread.

The English and Irish spinneries lead the world; they produce most of its lace thread. One of them, the Coates firm of Paisley, has established in Belgium branches in which Belgian capital is interested,—at Gent are the *filteries,* which prepare thread for weaving, and at Alost and Ninove are the *filatures* or spinneries which turn out the finished sewing and embroidery thread. The cottons and linens of these mills are too coarse for the delicate laces; however, during a single war year, the Brussels Committee was happy to be able to buy from Alost as much as 600,000 francs worth of thread. By some miracle, the Ghent filteries escaped the practically universal ruin visited on mills and factories, and should be operating before peace is signed, but for the spinneries of Alost and Ninove, the future is still dark.

During two years the enemy, feeling they might one day run the mills where they stood, left them intact, tho they requisitioned their stocks of thread. Then as they saw they might not perhaps be able to continue their beneficent occupation of Belgium, even if they won the war, they began to remove the mill machinery to Germany. They were especially ruthless when the mills were known to be of English or French ownership. They stole the secrets of the factories and finally they deported the workmen. These men are scattered everywhere. Even if the machines of the factories were not completely destroyed it would be impossible under a considerable time to reassemble the skilled workmen essential to the spinning industry. The Germans will undoubtedly try to capture the trade, and to market their goods, if they must, through such neutral countries as Denmark and Switzerland.

When I arrived at Courtrai, Monsieur and his family were just moving back into the house from which they had been ejected. They apologized for the room they so hospitably offered me, in which the original bed had been replaced by an iron one they recognized as having belonged to an English family of Courtrai. The brass trimmings were gone, and the mattress had of course been removed, but Madame had been able to find one stuffed with sea-moss for me. The curtains were slashed, blocks of wood nailed to the once handsome walls, there were no lights, no metal knobs or fixtures of any kind, no service wires left. Below, the cellar had been almost filled with concrete to provide the conqueror a safe refuge during danger periods. It requires a special kind of courage to take up life again in a place like this, but these good people said: "We can not complain, we are so much better off than others, and at least we have saved our health; with that we can be sure of being able to build again what they have destroyed."

From there I went to Baron de Bethune, a connoisseur of laces, who had before the war opened a lace museum in Courtrai, chiefly for Valenciennes. I found him ill in a little house in the town; he had long before been driven from his château in the suburbs. His sister, who had with great difficulty made her way from Louvain, received me with apologies in the midst of a heterogeny of boxes and packages, the few personal possessions they had gathered together in the hope of some day having a home again. I was not to see the old Valenciennes and other specimens of the famous lace days of Courtrai; fortunately for his museum, Monsieur had succeeded in getting them to Brussels where they were still, to my personal regret, hidden away. However, I was not surprized, for I had been unable before starting for Flanders to see the celebrated collection of the Cinquantenaire Museum at Brussels, for that, too, had been successfully secreted. Museums are slow in rehanging their treasures. Even tho the presence of the three neutral Ministers, the Spanish, American and Dutch, in the capital, was supposed to be a guaranty of protection to the national collections, and undoubtedly it was only their presence that prevented in Belgium what happened to the Museums of Northern France, the Belgians with unwearying ingenuity concealed what they could. Whenever I hear of hidden laces, I am reminded of a morning at Malines and a sad little basket containing a fine collection of old Malines lace, I saw exhumed. It had been buried deep in a box, along with the family silver, and as the daughter of the mother who had worn it took its once lovely flowers and webs, now gray and earth-stained, between her fingers, they powdered to dust.

Monsieur suggested that I see Mlle. Mullie, a leading dealer of Courtrai, who still handles a large output of Valenciennes; tho Courtrai, which was once a brilliant production center, is no longer of great importance. After the French Revolution, which killed Valenciennes-making in its original home, it migrated to other parts of Northern France, and to the two Flanders; to Ypres, where it enjoyed an especially happy development, to Bruges, Ghent, Dixmude, Furnes, Menin, Nieuport, Poperinghe and elsewhere. For a long time Ghent led all these, with over 5,000 workers listed in 1756. But starvation wages and successful imitations have told against this, as against other laces. Nevertheless, in the census of 1896, Bruges was still credited with 2,000 Valenciennes workers, and Poperinghe with 500, while there were scattered groups of considerable importance in a great number of the villages of Western, and some of Eastern Flanders.

Courtrai and the nearby villages where the lace is actually made, still stand, tho many buildings have been destroyed, but while her people were not forced to become refugees, lace-making was seriously interrupted; workers were evicted from their homes and their schools. And they suffered further because there was scarcely any thread left, the dealers often asking as much as 20 cents for ¾ of a yard of lace thread, about the previous value of the same length in finished lace. Under these conditions it was especially easy to see the importance of the efforts of the Brussels Lace Committee, which furnished thread at the normal price, and gave more for the lace than was ever offered before the war.

Unfortunately the German facteurs

BOBBIN LACES

First column: Malines, Malines, Point de Paris, Point de Paris, Valenciennes (square mesh)
Middle column: Point de Paris
Third column: First three, Valenciennes; fourth, Point de Paris

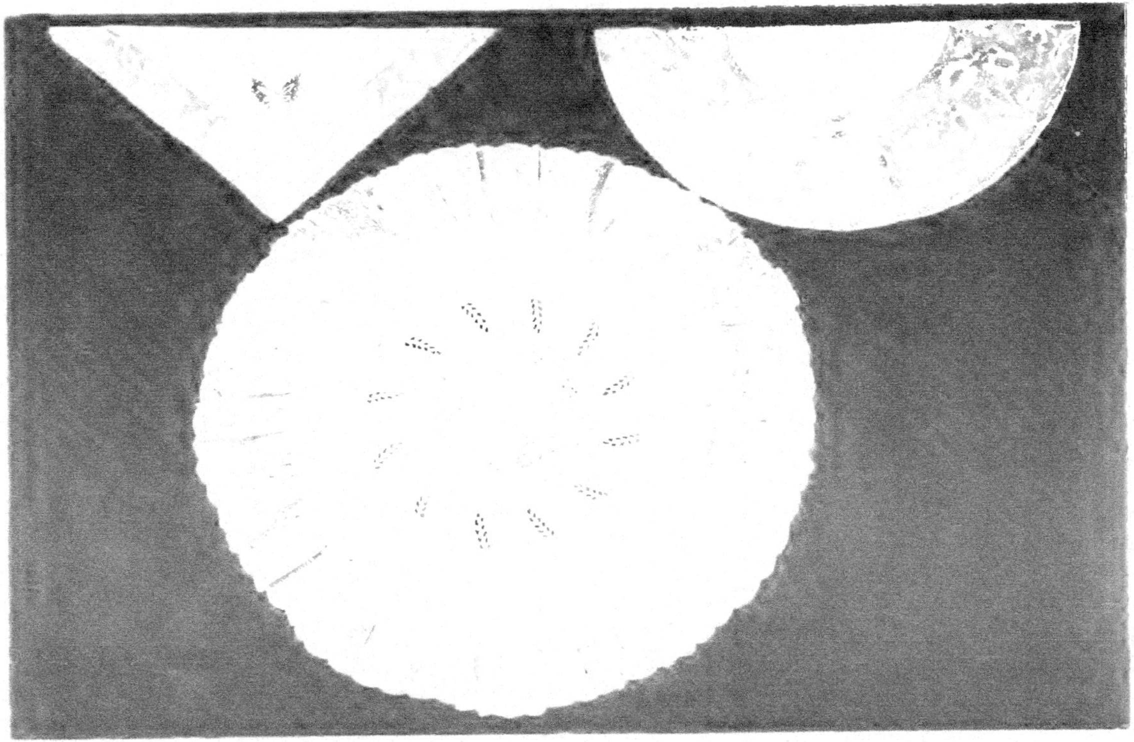

CUSHION COVER REPRESENTING BELGIUM'S GRATITUDE TO AMERICA FOR BREAD

Point de Paris lace combined with linen. The lower right-hand centerpiece shows the rose design, emblem of Queen Elizabeth (agents for lace dealers) worked cleverly here, too, as in other districts. They had always plenty of requisitioned thread to offer, and succeeded in buying considerable lace, for which they offered high and varying prices.

The younger women of the Courtrai region have been rapidly giving up Valenciennes to make Cluny, which pays better. A Valenciennes beginner, for example, must work a year as an apprentice, during which time she is able to earn scarcely more than five cents a day. The wages of the good workers have advanced, but unless they can be increased even more, there are few who will continue to make this difficult lace.

After 60 years' experience in lace, and latterly she has employed 1,000 women, Mlle. Mullie says that one is fortunate, among 5,000 workers, to find five who can execute a sample from a drawing not already interpreted or pricked for the worker. Before the war there were two good piqueuses in Ypres to whom Courtrai sent her difficult patterns, but only one of these still lives.

In peace-time the greater part of this Courtrai lace goes to Paris (some is sent to New York), which is all one needs to say in tribute to its pattern and its quality. Paris knows lace better than any other city in the world; she accepts only the best. We were talking of the 60 per cent. duty the United States Government levies on imported laces, and the harm it works to the Belgian industry. "That is our greatest discouragement, but there are other Government stupidities," Mlle. Mullie smiled. "France, for instance, charges 10½ francs on a kilo of Valenciennes, and the same amount on an equal weight of Cluny; the Valenciennes may be worth several thousand, and the Cluny three or four francs!"

The true old Valenciennes mesh, called

"Rond," is still made at Courtrai, as well as at Bruges; the modern Valenciennes commonly has a square mesh, which is preferred by many connoisseurs, since it is more transparent and sets the flowers off more strikingly. "Whether or not you prefer it to the square, you must see the traditional round Valenciennes mesh," Mlle. Mullie said, and we started off in the rain for a group of tiny brick houses, the Gottshuisen (God's houses) which the city furnishes free to certain old people.

Before we reached the first, I saw two white heads near a window, bending over cushions; and once inside, on those cushions, lengths of snowy Valenciennes of the old round mesh, of an admirable regularity and loveliness. These two women were both over 70 years old, and they sat before their bobbins, twisting and braiding the eight threads of the mesh as they had twisted and braided them for over a half century, and still cheerfully hoping that they might some day win more than 15 or 20 cents a day for their work. "Now we must have more," they said gently, "because thread and oil are so much more expensive than they were before the war."

In the next house, the old woman whose sister was ill could afford no light at all; when dusk fell she had to leave her bobbin mounds and her mesh and flowers and go to bed—what else could she do without coal or oil?

It was the last day of 1918, and I decided that Mrs. Bayard Henry of Philadelphia, who had sent me a little money to use as I chose, would be happy to give to these sweet, faithful women and their thirteen neighbors, candles and oil as hope symbols for the New Year. I left her gift with Mlle. Mullie.

It was already very late, and I had not time to go to Wevelghem and Gulleghem, two of the most important lace-villages contributing to Courtrai. Mlle. Mullie was facing the future with courage. "I am sure," she said, "that Peat, from whom I have bought thread for forty years, will not forget me, and that I may be able to count on a shipment from England at a just price as soon as anything can come through. That I have been cut off during four years will make no difference. I shall write, too, to a friend in France, and from Puy I may have a few skeins. The question of pins and bobbins is serious—they seem to have disappeared, and one can not start a worker on less than a dozen bobbins. Those I have thus far succeeded in finding cost 95 centimes the dozen, as against the 28 centimes of pre-war times. There seem literally to be no pins. However, despite everything, I, at least, hope to see my thousand women at some not too distant time again busy over their cushions.

A few have already sought me out to let me know they are ready, waiting only for the precious thread. I regret infinitely the passing of the fine 'Val,' but we shall continue to produce as much as we can, and at any rate we shall try unceasingly to raise the standard of the Clunys and Torchons."

III

THOUROUT — THIELT — WYNGHENE

III

THOUROUT—THIELT—WYNGHENE

In the Important Bobbin Lace Area

ON a spring-like Saturday in early January, I left Bruges by the Thourout road for Thielt. As I turned beyond the Porte, I found myself speeding toward the great arms of one of those Dutch windmills that so frequently, in the lowlands, close the long vista. The farther I rode into the Thourout region, the more it seemed the loveliest bit of Western Flanders I had yet seen. The gentle outlines of the low red brick farmhouses followed with satisfying harmony the landscape contours. Farm succeeded farm in swift succession, small farms, where every square foot of soil was green with sprouting grain or vegetables, and in the morning sunlight the thickly sown cottages shone like jewels on the plain.

Pink and white geraniums blossomed behind many of the quaint windows, and I knew that near them grandmothers, or mothers, or daughters (or possibly all three together) were sitting before their cushions, and from pin to pin were twisting and braiding Cluny and Duchesse, the characteristic laces of this section. This was an excellent day for lace-making with its sunshine of summer.

To the south and east of the badly shelled town of Thourout, I visited the districts of Iseghem, Thielt and Wynghene, all celebrated for their guipures. Guipure, a rather vague commercial term covering two widely different groups of lace, may be loosely defined as bobbin lace without a mesh base. One group of guipures includes the Clunys (named after the Cluny museum in Paris because they employ many old Gothic designs) which are made in one length or piece. They closely resemble the more common Torchons, surpassing them, however, in fineness and firmness of execution, and in brilliancy of design—the distinguishing connecting bars of Cluny often throw the figures into conspicuous relief. While this one-piece lace is usually made of the coarser threads, fine linen or cotton, or even silk thread, is also employed. In the second group of guipures are those made in separate small bits, or details, which are afterward joined to make the flounce or piece, the most common of these varieties being Flanders and Duchesse. In the schools of Thielt and Wynghene all the kinds are taught. Because they are made of coarser thread and therefore more quickly than such laces as Valenciennes or Needle Point, are less taxing to the eyes, and pay better, these guipures have gained ground in almost every lace center in Belgium, and often threaten the very existence of the finer laces. If it had not been for the leadership of the "Amies de la Dentelle," of a few of the more intelligent and disinterested dealers, and above all of certain convents to whom Belgium owes the preservation of many of her finest designs and varieties, it is a question if any but the few remaining old women, who for forty or fifty years have preferred to follow one pattern, would still produce the old meshes and points. Much hope now centers in the corrective influence of the recently founded Normal School at Bruges and of the other schools of Belgium, but, despite all the efforts of these combined groups, delicate laces like the Malines have been fast disappearing.

The little farmhouse, if one can call two rooms a house, I visited on the edge of Thielt demonstrated clearly what is happening. It was Saturday afternoon and the mother of the large family of boys at play on the neat brick path outside, was scrubbing the tiled floor, moving the small baskets of potatoes and heaps of tobacco leaves and sabots and the winter sled from place to place as she proceeded. The socks to be darned, each already a fantastic patch-work, were piled on the window-sill, where there was room beside for a geranium and a fern. The stove and the table were also crowded into this, the general living-room, which despite all attempts to arrange things, boasted scarcely one unincumbered foot of floor space. However, over near the window with its two plants, were the customary chair and the cushion, and the girl of sixteen, absorbed in her lace, quite oblivious of the water her mother was splashing about her feet.

The adjoining room was similarly

crowded; it had to serve as bedroom for this large family. There was the mantelpiece with the familiar row of bright plates and vases,—the place where the family's art sense finds concentrated expression. Fortunately, this room, too, had a window with other plants, and before it sat the grandmother in her black cap and shawl, who, as I entered, was just slipping her battered eye-glasses into the little side drawer beneath her cushion. She smiled a friendly greeting, and uncovered her lace, a filmy flounce of Valenciennes about four inches wide, firm and regular, and of a good old design. She had been making Valenciennes all her life; she would make it to the end. She was delighted to show me how she twisted four threads to form one side of the hexagon of the mesh, and four to form the opposite, and the union points where the eight met. Then she held up a length of her lace and told us that a facteur (neighborhood buyer for a large business house) had been there just before we arrived, to try to buy her flounce at nine francs the *aune,* which would be roughly, about $2.50 a meter. The committee has been giving her 19 fr. 50 c. ($3.90) for the same amount, and she asked anxiously, tho still smilingly, if she might not continue to hope for the committee price, even tho the war had stopt. It is pathetic, day after day, to hear that question repeated, and not yet to be certain of the answer. However, one can always reply truthfully, that the women of the "Friends of the Lace" will work unceasingly not only to hold wages where they are, but to advance them.

I turned from this delicate lace to the granddaughter's cushion—she was making guipure de Cluny, of coarse linen thread. Marie's pattern happened to be a good one and she was working swiftly and evenly, sure of a fair day's wage.

Here, then, was a suggestive contrast, and however one may regret it, it exists in the large majority of lace-making households in Belgium, and is only to be expected. It is but the deserved penalty of a past and present economic blindness or callousness. Where they are not making Cluny, the younger women of this district give their time to ordinary varieties of guipure which they call Bruges and Milan, or Point de Bruges, and Point de Milan.

While I had been watching the Valenciennes and Cluny, the mother of the household, who had the mop of fuzzy dark red hair often seen in this region, had hurried her scrubbing to an end, and wiping her hands on her blue apron, was ready to uncover her own cushion. I looked at the chapped, rough skin and the hands used to pulling weeds and digging potatoes and scrubbing, and realized that they could not possibly hold a piece

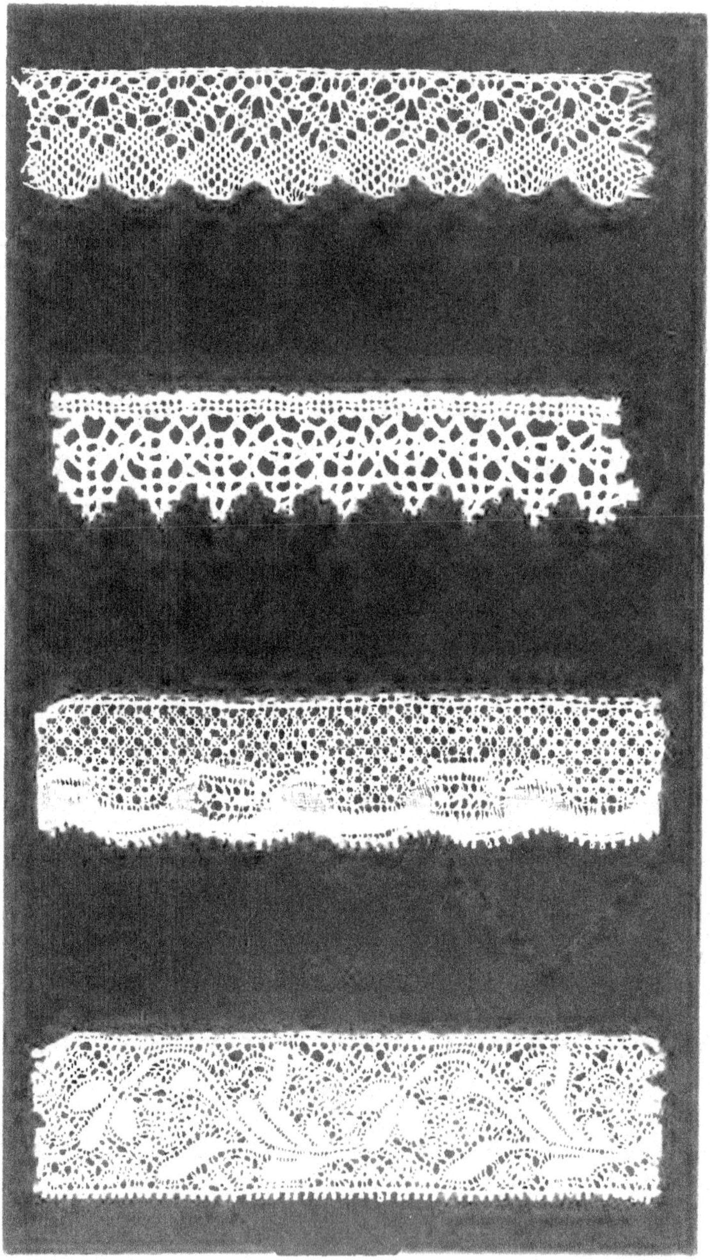

BOBBIN LACES

(1) Torchon (2) Cluny (3) Old Flemish (4) Binche

TABLE CLOTH SHOWING ARMS OF THE ALLIES

Cut linen with squares of Venise surrounded by filet and cluny. Venise made with the needle, cluny with bobbins of fine sewing—the thread would catch with every stitch—and yet that she could turn from her scrubbing-brush to the little wooden bobbins (her fingers need not touch the thread) and proceed without difficulty on a snowy bit of Valenciennes—for happily she was following her mother in Valenciennes.

There are three schools in Thielt, of which the convent schools de la Charité and de l'Espérance are the more important. I went first to the Convent de la Charité, with Mlle. van der Graeht, who has throughout the war been devoted to the workers and the lace. Tho Thielt lay in the danger zone, she refused to choose a safer city, remaining to share the work of her father, who added to his arduous duties as administrator of the *arrondisement,* those of the representative of the Brussels Lace Committee. Two weeks before the end, however, the Germans drove these patriots from their house (three bombs from Allied aeroplanes had already fallen on it) and they were denied the experience they had been waiting for throughout all the years, that of seeing the Allied soldiers march into Thielt. One of the Germans was frank enough to tell them that they were being forced away chiefly to prevent their "assisting" at that deliverance.

Immediately after the armistice they returned, and installed themselves comfortably once more on the first floor of their almost roofless house. When I arrived they had not yet come in from their first inspection trip of the communes just behind the lines, and I was welcomed by pretty, brown-haired Flavia and her six-year-old Albert. Flavia's husband had been killed at the front during the first months of the war, and she had served in this household throughout all its terrible duration. As I looked from the windows of the drawing-room, still intact, across the rear garden, to the mass of wreckage that was once the neighboring house, I understood the feeling of the impotence of all effort produced by the casualness of these bombs, that spare here to strike there, and why in the war one inevitably becomes a fatalist. And as I looked across the garden, Flavia told me something of her experience with the thirteen Germans who took over the house when they drove her master out and of how whenever the shelling was severe they ran to the cellars, and several times tried to persuade her to go with them but she always refused. "I preferred," she said, "to die alone with my little boy in the open, to risking being killed with them in the cellar." On Sunday, October 13, between 11 and 2 o'clock, sixty shells fell on Thielt, and all day Monday and the following days they continued to fall, until on Saturday the 19th, the French marched into the town.

To add to the horror of this period, people were dying in large numbers of influenza. Flavia told me of the street-sweeper who died at the corner with her broom in her hand. By some miracle she and her little boy escaped both shell and pestilence, and when Monsieur and his daughter returned they found her scrubbing and restoring as best she could after the flight of the enemy. This was one of the centers where during the four terror-years a bright beacon burned for all the surrounding territory, for it was here that the people of the villages and the convents could bring their laces for the committee, knowing they would be accepted and paid for. In 1916, the Baron van der Graeht was encouraging the work in no less than seventeen communes and of as many as 3,500 lace-workers. Flavia smiled as she remembered something—"What good luck, there will be a sister coming this very day about 2 o'clock, with her laces." As she said this, the door opened—father and daughter were back from their pony-cart expedition to the front-lines.

Monsieur was still visibly moved by what he had seen, even after his own four years' experience. "Madame," he said, "I can not describe my emotion on going about in those little shattered villages just behind the lines, where the women have insisted on remaining, and where day by day, and year after year, they have sat calmly before their cushions making lace, while the shells burst before and behind them. After such a victory as theirs, the lace industry of Belgium must live."

Mademoiselle gave me the list of the badly destroyed villages, and then the names of those which had suffered less and that, with Thielt, produced the most lace. Among them were Pittham and Ardois (which specializes in old Bruges);

Ruysselede (with an excellent school for Valenciennes), Aerseele, and Maria Loop. Thielt, itself, had at the beginning of 1919 about 300 workers, of whom a hundred were in the school of the convent de l'Espérance, and about 60 in the Convent de la Charité. There had been times of great discouragement; in one particularly dark hour in 1917 many of the workers had turned back to the old facteurs, or village agents, for help, and unfortunately some of these sold to the Germans, who were constantly trying to win them by offering large sums for their laces. Since he was under no obligation to turn over a fixt wage to the workers, the facteur might reap any profit he could secure.

We abandoned this unpleasant subject to talk of the schools, the hope of the future, and after lunch I went with Mlle. to visit one of these, the Convent de la Charité, on the edge of the town, with its

60 girls, who have supplied the committee with much old Flanders and Cluny. Even tho this was a Saturday afternoon in winter, 45 of the 60 chairs were occupied by girls between 12 and 16. One rarely finds a girl over 18 in the schools; once she has learned her trade, she prefers to work at home with the mother and grandmother.

Unfortunately in this, which is considered a "good" school for Flanders, I found the longest hours I had yet met, that is, summer hours. In winter, because of the poor light, they are shorter. It seems unbelievable, but the sisters told me that in summer the children come at 5:30 o'clock and work until 8 at night —with only three half-hours for recreation—one at 8.30 o'clock, one at 12, and one at 4. A day of 13 hours for growing children, and girls who are maturing! It is such cruel conditions as these that the Committee have done their best to ameliorate. In this case, tho the hours are still criminal, the wages have been improved.

However, "improved wages" leave much still to be fought for. I talked with a girl of twelve in the front row, an apprentice, and found that she earns between 40 and 50 centimes a day, or about 10 cents for her 13 hours' labor, which tho it is almost double what she could have earned before the war, is nevertheless only 10 cents per day. The Committee was able to add the war-time subsidy of 20 per cent. to this. Naturally, the learner can not yet make what is called good lace, and unfortunately her parents are often only too content to have her bring home 10 cents a day. The older, more experienced girls, were earning from one to two francs a day, or from 20 to 40 cents, that is, on a summer's day or full day.

Monsieur told me later that in his region if the wage of the good worker can be raised to 50 cents per day, she will be able to live, and will be content to remain at home before her lace cushion rather than to go to the shoe and cotton factories of Thielt.

The advanced pupils were eager to uncover their treasure. Nearly all of them had protected their round cushions with a circular piece of thick blue glazed paper, with a hole in the middle. Through the hole they worked with their rather heavy cherry wood bobbins, on the meshless guipures of Cluny and Bruges and Flanders, which this school prefers. Several were finishing the collar and cuff sets of rather coarse but pretty Bruges with its characteristic rose and trefoil, seen so commonly in shop windows, and which are especially effective when worn with cotton or linen frocks. The Guipure de Flandres pupils were making square insets for table and tray-cloths of simple, geometric designs. Two girls were at work on what they called Guipure de Milan, of a wide spreading branch and flower pattern.

However, the most interesting lace was not the guipure but the Point de Flandres or Old Flanders, with its elaborate mesh base, just now experiencing an interesting and encouraging revival, in which the zealous Baron van der Graeht felt Thielt should assist. A half-dozen older girls were executing doily and table center rounds in this lace, after the Committee's very popular Swan pattern. They were using a fairly coarse linen thread, and working the rich, solid mesh with eight bobbins. "Whoever would make the Old Flanders mesh must be willing to play a game of patience," Madame had once said to me. The dull, plain woven parts of the pattern are brilliantly outlined by a still coarser thread, and in the "jours" or open-work spaces are the much loved snow-balls characteristic of Binche lace. Because of its combined strength and beauty, there could hardly be a more successful lace for general use than this Old Flanders, sometimes called Antik.

While it was once the most generally made and most celebrated of Flemish bobbin laces (it was known in every part of Flanders in 1500), it had been almost forgotten for generations, but even tho it has been little remembered for some time, Old Flanders may be said never to have died. In certain regions, that of Antwerp for instance, it is found continuously on the garments of priests. It is the lace that remained always at the base and from which the other bobbin laces, from time to time, sprang. It is to be hoped that the Committee's laudable effort to revive it will bear increasing rewards.

Tho they could understand no French,

and I knew only a few words of Flemish, these little and big girls found much amusement in my visit, and in my inability to follow their swift fingers. These were fingers accustomed, too, to weed the fields and to dig potatoes, for there is practically no lace made here during the weeks of August and September when the potato-crop is gathered. The Sisters of Charity, teachers in this school, were poor themselves, as their surroundings testified. They had no fine carved oak armoire for their laces, but brought from some safe place a tin box, like an ordinary bread-box, in which were the dainty white packets ready to be sent to the Committee at Brussels. As they were exhibiting piece after lovely piece, they unfolded the swan pattern doily rounds of Old Flanders, and after a moment's hesitation, Sister A. ventured, "There is one thing you might do for us, Madame; when you return to Brussels, could you not tell the Committee that while the small swan doily rounds are sufficiently paid, this large centerpiece round is not? It is our fault in estimating; we did not realize how long it would take to make it." I could not resist teasing them a little and replied that I should be delighted to carry the message were it not for the fact that it was precisely this set of swan doilies (as it was) that the Committee had given me for Christmas. "Should you like me to tell them," I asked, "that they had not paid enough for my present?" They were covered with confusion, as I expected they would be, and then how they laughed, those frail little sisters. "*Mais,* Madame, that would indeed be difficult; we will write; we had forgotten. *Non,* Madame, you certainly could not tell them that! But we can write letters now whenever we wish—can we not? One loses the habit in four years." And then they laughed again all together.

It was already late when I reached Wynghene. The shell-pitted roads of western Flanders had made all my traveling difficult and I could not see Mlle. Slock, one of the rare lace dealers who has looked beyond her immediate purse and has taken time to revive old models and invent new ones, seeking in every way to raise the standard of the present production in all her region, which is chiefly devoted to Cluny. I had not time to stop in the village, but hurried on beyond it to a cheerful red brick manor house set in a forest, the home of the Burgomaster of Wynghene, whose wife has been the untiringly devoted representative of the Committee for this section.

As we sat at tea together, near the conservatory windows, where we could look through the naked garden trees across a meadow to the forest beyond, the Burgomaster told me of the morning when they stood at these windows, after the shells had been falling for days all about them, waiting and watching, scarcely daring to breathe, and of how as they watched, he saw through the trees of the forest what looked like a brown shadow, but the brown shadow moved, and then running across the meadow, where he had always believed they must break through, came the Belgian soldiers, the soldiers of deliverance. "I know our hearts stopt beating; we stood choking, incapable of motion, as we watched them come—still unable to believe after four years of waiting."

We were silent for a few minutes, then we began to talk of the lace. As his wife turned to get the list of her villages, I asked if the Germans had attempted to get her workers away from her. "They had their agents here, as everywhere," she answered, "and I regret to admit that one of their most successful ones was a Belgian woman, who had been a facteur, or lace gatherer for larger houses, before the war. When the Germans offered her large prices, she consented to serve them. If she had been sacrificing herself for what she believed to be the good of the workers, we might have forgiven her, but it was obvious that she was not—she is pretty and likes pretty clothes—*Voila tout!* Along with several other disloyal citizens, she was imprisoned the other day, but unfortunately after only twenty-four hours, succeeded in freeing herself. However, the people will never forget that she trafficked with the enemy."

I had known of the German lace organization first through seeing the huge sign, "*Allgemeine Spitzen Centrale*" (Central lace depot), just across from our C. R. B. offices. And as soon as I got in touch with the loyal work of the women of the

Belgian Lace Committee, I was daily hearing of this or that attempt of their oppressors to capture the designs and the output of the country. They might succeed with the simpler, more helpless workers, who because of their great misery may be forgiven for selling to them—and with the deserters and activists—but they were daily defeated by the Committee patriots. I was thoroughly interested to hear, now, from one of the patriots, that the idea of the German "Lace Control" possibly had its birth in Wynghene. In February, 1915, a certain Freiherr Von Rippenhausen was stationed at Wynghene. He had with him his young American wife—they had been married but a short time, and the people of the village were kind enough to say they believed she was not German by conviction! However that may be, the Von Rippenhausens requisitioned lodgings in the house of one of the lace buyers of Wynghene, and in this house they naturally discovered much regarding the lace situation, the lack of thread, and the distress of the workers, and of the Belgian system by which the facteur furnishes the thread to the worker and buys the finished products, which he in turn sells to a big lace house, reaping what profit he can as intermediary. Frau von Rippenhausen, in particular, informed herself thoroughly, and together she and her husband, it is said, organized the German "Lace Control," with headquarters at Brussels.

Since the Germans had requisitioned all the thread they could lay their hands on, of which there were enormous stocks in Belgium, it was not difficult for them to offer it to the workers. They sent German soldier facteurs into every corner of the country to offer large prices to native facteurs or to individual workers. On receiving a piece of lace, they supplied an equal weight of thread to the workers, thus establishing a continuing chain of material and product. And they claimed to be selling their lace in America! They were clever enough to profit, in 1917, by the Committee's apparent inability to go on at that moment, exercising every pressure they could, and naturally they gained ground. No one can say yet how much lace they were able to buy, but the amount of inferior lace was considerable.

Madame Van der Bruggen's records show that before 1917 there were in Wynghene, contributing to the Committee, 400 workers on Cluny and Duchesse, about 200 on Cluny and Valenciennes in Beernem, 200 on Valenciennes in Oedelem, and 350 in Oostcamp, all grateful to have the Committee's fixt minimum of three francs' work a week insured to them. Some of these villages, Beernem and Oostcamp for instance, are usually included in the Bruges district.

She praised the Committee's method of raising the wage by standardizing the values of certain designs as executed by an average worker; the poorer workers then gained less, the superior ones, more. "I thought I realized," she said, "how cruelly underpaid our women were, but it was not until I saw their joy when the Committee promised them that at least they should always have a minimum of ten centimes an hour for their work, that I really understood. Ten centimes (two cents), just a postage stamp, for a whole hour's straining effort; and they were happy because that was so much more than they had been sure of winning before the war!"

IV

GRAMMONT

IV

GRAMMONT

Belgian Home of Chantilly

THE Committee was discouraging about Grammont. When I told Madame de Beughem of my plan to go there to see Chantilly lace in the making, she answered, "But that will be a futile journey; the women have had practically no black or white silk thread since the war, and the few who were still working in 1914 will have stopt; that one-time important branch of the industry has almost ceased to exist." I decided, however, to visit the tomb of Chantilly, the lace so closely identified with Grammont that in Belgium it takes its name from that city, rather than from its original French home.

And Grammont itself, a town of 13,000 inhabitants, was well worth the journey, situated as it is in a lovely region of rolling hills, and deriving its name from the steep slope (Grand Mont) to which part of the city clings. The surrounding undulating country is dotted with quaint, clustered villages, some with thatched, some with tiled roofs, and only twenty miles away is the charming town of Audenarde—poor Audenarde, so cruelly wounded by the war!

I reached Grammont about noon, having lost an hour on the way through the difficulty of passing camions and artillery and marching companies of Canadian soldiers. Between Ninove and Grammont, too, were many squads of German prisoners at work on the ruined road. They were guarded by the French, but it was a rather lenient surveillance, at any rate

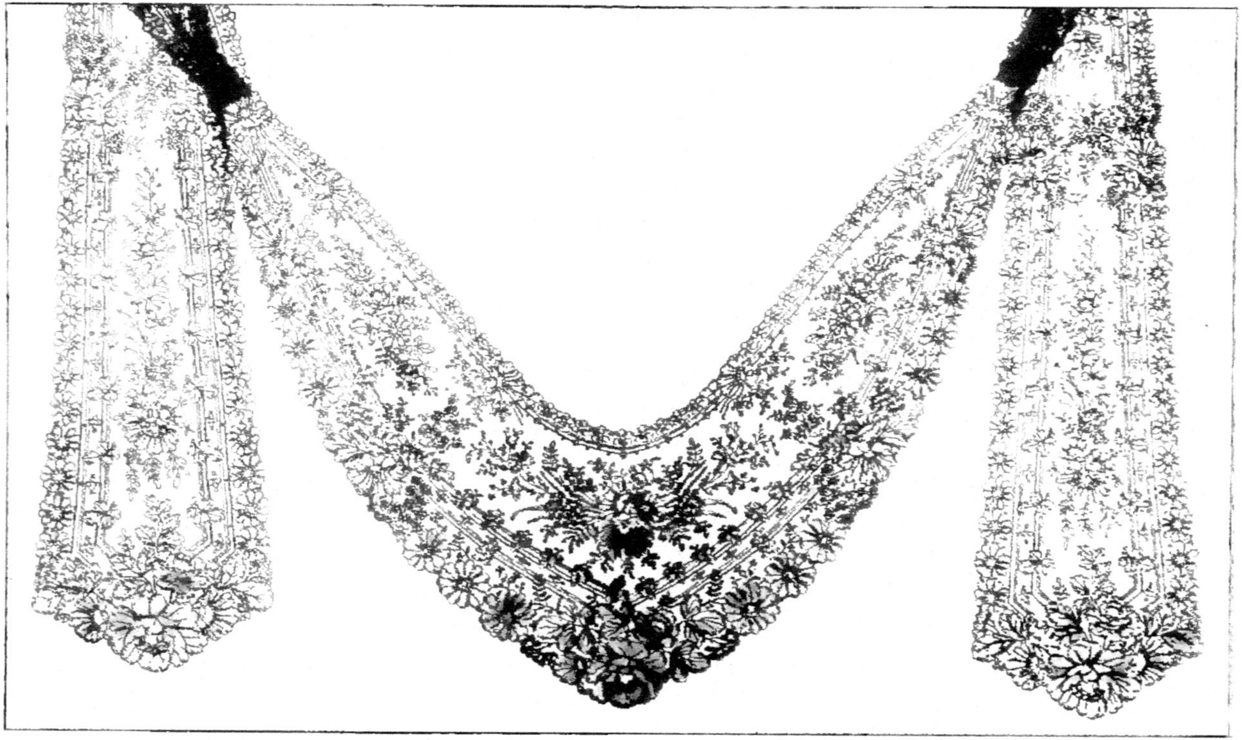

A "MARIE ANTOINETTE" IN CHANTILLY LACE, MADE WITH BOBBINS, NEAR GRAMMONT

CUSHION COVER

Center Venise, borders Valenciennes, lace executed by 12 workers in one month, embroidery and mounting by four women in two months, design by M. de Rudder

TEA CLOTH

Point de E

the sullen groups in their trailing gray capes appeared to be casually tapping the mud with their spades instead of being genuinely at work.

My Belgian chauffeur, whose health is broken after three years of forced labor in Germany, would have been delighted to run them down, and at one point did succeed in splashing a group with mud, as he called "Boches" and something I did not catch. I began to understand the ruling that released Belgian prisoners shall not be placed over Germans still held here.

After lunch I started with Madame Cuseners to the little lace school whose director has courageously carried on during the four years. We walked through a narrow arched passageway beside a brick building and into a large hall at the rear which was at one time the lace classroom. Instead of lace-workers, however, we found Scotch and Canadian soldiers busy tacking the Union Jack and Belgian flags on the wall, and hanging boughs and festoons of colored paper rings—they were making ready for a "grand" New Year's Eve dancing party. In the courtyard still farther back a half-dozen Scotchmen had built a campfire, protecting it with a low canvas roof, and it was burning brightly despite the dismal rain.

It shone on the windows of the long, narrow room at the side of the court, which looked like a conservatory, but which had become the refuge of the lace-workers, when because of lack of thread and fuel, they could no longer occupy their hall. I found fifty sweet-faced girls between thirteen and fifteen busy over their cushions, a faithful, tired-looking old Abbé and an enthusiastic young woman teacher. They were not making black nor the less important white silk Chantilly, for they had long been entirely without silk thread. Nevertheless, they were preserving the art of making it, since they had been kept at work on Chantilly designs executed with bobbins and the white cotton thread furnished by the Committee. They had some fine flounces, which were not, however, to be compared with the traditional black silk ones of the great Chantilly days.

For Chantilly has seen great days. It appeared first in France about 1740, where it achieved a phenomenal popularity, which was unfortunately rudely ended by the Revolution, for since it was a favorite lace at court, the Revolutionists made it a crime to appear in Chantilly. Later, under the Empire, it enjoyed a revival, the fabrication of the silk laces spread in France; Bayeux became a celebrated center; and, finally, toward 1835, it crossed to Belgium, where Grammont was early recognized as its home. In 1851 all of the forty-nine schools of that province taught the technique of this lace. Then toward 1870 true Chantilly seemed doomed a second time to extinction by the success of the machine imitations of St. Pierre des Calais, and also because the vogue for black lace had passed. But again the pendulum has swung back; the imitations are now greatly in favor and there is a cheering increase in the demand for the true lace flounces.

The Abbé brought out from dusty drawers the school's stock of designs, elegant groupings of bouquets and foliage, with occasional striking geometrical details introduced, all joined by a fine hexagonal mesh, which resembled at first that of Malines, and later, more closely, the Point d'Alencon mesh. The fact that this lace is often used for scarfs and gowns, and that the customary flounce is of generous width, has encouraged the development of elaborate patterns. Some of the sketches were divided by heavy pencil lines into the separate narrow strips on which the lace-maker actually works. To achieve the wide flounce, these strips are attached one to another by special workers who employ a joining stitch that defies detection. The individual pattern strips include both mesh and flowers and follow irregular lines, curving, it may be, to include a full-petaled rose. When one examines the fineness of the clear hexagonal mesh that forms the base of Chantilly, it seems all the more remarkable that the division lines are not visible. This Chantilly mesh has differed during various periods and besides there are always almost as many varieties as there are workers, for one weaves more closely or more firmly than another. I came soon to realize how great a difference in effect results from a practically invisible variation in the thickness of the thread, or in the manner of twisting or looping it or in the placing of the pins. One of the distinguishing characteristics of Chantilly is the relief produced by a heavier thread that outlines the pattern and forms the twigs and veins of the leaves. In securing a brilliant relief, the French have always succeeded better than the Belgians.

These Grammont pupils were also making Blonde, a favorite lace with the Spanish people, and introduced into Belgium from France at the same time as Chantilly. Its processes are very similar, tho it is easily differentiated from its sister by the heavy glossy petals of its flowers and their conspicuous open-work centers in the Point de Paris stitch. The name Blonde is derived from the écru silk which was first employed in its making; now it is made of white or of black silk, and chiefly in the form of scarfs or mantillas. The girls were making their war-time Blonde of cotton, the good Peat cotton of Nottingham, brought in by the C. R. B. for the Lace Committee. It is practically only in the Grammont and Turnhout regions that Blonde is still made.

The instructress showed me the little bundles of poor, crooked brass pins that were all that remained after four years of the occupation, explaining what harm poor pins can work in a fine mesh like that of Chantilly. Then she asked if I could not tell them when they might expect new ones. Alas, these disheartening months of the winter of 1918-1919 when one hope after another has been deferred; so many things to be done at once, and all depending on the re-establishment of a system of transportation utterly destroyed.

I went from the school-room, past the fire in the courtyard, back to the large hall where the Canadians were still decorating for their party, and where we wished one another a Happy New Year—brave Canadian boys well loved by the Belgians —then on to the house of Madame's mother, who for a half-century has been a lace *fabricant,* or dealer, and whose front room served easily as combined salon and office. Precious laces need very little space; they can be stored in a handsome carved oak armoire, which is at once a safe and a beautiful article of furniture. This old lady's hair was still dark and glossy, as is so often the case with grandmothers in Europe, and her brown eyes were bright and keen. She talked of the time when there were more than twenty dealers employing over 2,000 workers on Chantilly in the Grammont region, and of the gradual decline of the industry. "Certain empty houses on the heights above the town tell the story. Long ago the lace-makers left the valley at the foot of the slope, and seeking the brighter light on the hill, formed a lace colony there; but they have come down again, the houses on the hill are deserted. One by one the skilled old workers have died, and their secrets with them. There is only one really excellent piqueuse left and she is a baker-woman who exercises her talent of pricking patterns between baking! And I believe that instead of the former thousands, we have not more than eight hundred dentellières to-day. Here, as elsewhere, factories have come, and the lace has fled. With us it is the cigar and the match that have banished it, they furnish better wages and our women follow. However, if we can win a higher pay for the lace, and can but develop the little school you have just visited, and continue to train our girls, we shall yet be able to restore Chantilly. Especially," she added, "if we can be helped by that fickle Mistress Fashion, who last year smiled again on the black lace gown. Some of our patterns for robes can be made in a few weeks, but the truly fine ones take months, even a year to make. All depends on the design and the number of threads. We have had much to combat in the success of the marvelous Calais machine imitations of Chantilly, but true lovers of lace will never be content with them, however clever they are."

She shook out a folded triangular shawl. "There is no lace in the world more beautiful than this," she said, as she spread it on the white tablecloth, the better to display the wealth of its black flower clusters and long fronds, and then had me squeeze the delicate mesh in my hand to test its resiliency. I could not but agree with her. Her daughter brought out an exquisite collar, a tendril and flower pattern, with long tabs that could be crossed in front and let fall like a sash behind, a "Marie Antoinette" of most tempting loveliness; then a dainty parasol and a fan and a few filmy winged butterflies—all pieces made before the war, before the Germans set a wall of fire between the women of Grammont and the silk thread (Grenadine d'Alays) which meant their bread.

I was glad to have a few hours of sweeping hill country between these elegant black laces and the Valenciennes I was next to see; for the moment all white lace seemed negligible.

V

BRUGES

V

BRUGES

Queen of Lace Cities

AFTER a day beside the graves of Nieuport and Dixmude and Ypres, the first glimpse of the singing towers of Bruges against the evening sky seems an unearthly vision. During four years no one had known that Bruges would not perish as her sisters had perished. One must have come direct from the desolation of Nieuport, to her pignons and bridges, from the skeleton of Les Halles of Ypres to her Hôtel de Ville, to estimate her incomparable beauty. Since Ypres is dead, only Bruges and Turnhout remain as true lace cities of Belgium; Ghent, the elegant neighbor of

Bruges, and herself once a Queen in the lace world, has turned to her factories and no longer counts. Except Turnhout, then, with its famous schools for fine laces, no Belgian city to-day challenges the leadership of Bruges, and beyond Belgium, she has but one great rival—Venice

This claim to leadership rests on a solid foundation. Bruges is of ancient lineage in the lace world; she has preserved unbroken, through at least four centuries, the traditions of that world. There are those even who believe that medieval bobbin lace had its origin in her territory, and they are at least supported by legend. A pretty story tells of a poor and infirm widow, who with her many children lived in a little street of Bruges. The entire family depended only on the work of Serena, the eldest, who from dawn till dark turned her wheel. She had long been loved by a

LACE-MAKERS OF BRUGES

BRUGES AND SIMILAR BOBBIN LACES

First column: Bruges
Middle column: Bruges; Bruges, Bruges, Rosaline
Third Column: Rosaline, Old Flanders, Old Flanders, Duchesse

neighbor, Arnold, the son of a great merchant, and she did not view him with disfavor. But as winter and misery settled again on the poor little hut, and Serena saw that all her efforts appeared vain, she vowed to the Virgin never to marry unless her family could be rescued from their suffering. Then one day when near the Minnewater, as she was making sad thoughts, suddenly she saw a light, and from the Virgin threads descended toward her, which, skipping the branches, dropt in her lap, where they by chance designed lovely patterns. Serena understood this to be the response to her prayer, and she tried at once to reproduce the arabesques in linen thread. She ended by attaching little woods to them and by aiding them with pins. And thus to the great emotion of Bruges bobbin-lace was born. And all the rich seigneurs and bourgeois wished to possess it. Ease came and Serena married Arnold, and they had many daughters, all of whom she taught to make lace.

The often quoted picture in the Louvre Gallery, painted by Hans Memling (14— to 1494) and representing the Virgin and the Infant Christ surrounded by gift-bearers, among whom is a rich Brugeois wearing a gray costume trimmed with a bobbin-lace edging, certainly indicates that the industry existed in this epoch, and possibly had its center at Bruges, then the principal city in Flanders and the seat of the court. Furthermore, records prove that already at the opening of the 16th century, lace-making was included as a necessary part of the education of women. The edicts of Charles V requiring that it should be taught in all the schools and convents, greatly stimulated its development in Bruges, as well as throughout the entire Flanders and the provinces of Hainaut, Brabant and Antwerp. It became so popular an occupation for women that Charles's successor, Philip II, required that the magistrates of Ghent and Bruges restrict the number of lace-workers in their cities, in order that the rich might find some women left willing to serve them. Another enlightening document shows that in 1544 Bruges counted 7,696 poor among her population, and that the department of public charity required of the young women among them that they should cease to walk the streets and should learn the lace industry. There were at that time many lace schools. During the following centuries, Bruges maintained her position as a lace center and was able to survive the death-blow the French Revolution dealt the industry. For we find, about the middle of the 19th century, the city still counted seventy-nine schools, attended by 2,722 pupils, while in Valenciennes, for example, lace-making no longer existed.

There is, then, a rich and ancient past

back of the clicking bobbins of the Bruges of to-day. After four years of German rule it is still difficult to give accurate statistics, but generally speaking, in this city of 54,000 inhabitants, as many as 5,000 women and girls make lace of some sort. If you question the average woman, she will probably look at you in surprize and say: "How many lace-makers? Why, everybody; there is hardly a house in Bruges without its cushion and bobbins." While if you put the same question to such a celebrated lace dealer as M. Gillemont de Cock, who counts gold and silver medals from many nations, he will be very apt to answer: "Madame, before the war I knew of about thirty, now I can not say!" The Lace Committee at Brussels considers 5,000 a fair estimate for Bruges and her contributing villages, which is the number given, too, by Professor Maertens of the Normal School.

By the Bruges district is meant chiefly

Bruges, quite the contrary of the usual situation. One hears of the Alost region, for instance, and finds that while the villages of the surrounding area count thousands of workers, in the city of Alost itself very few are left. However, Bruges, too, counts some few outlying villages. Madame Ryeland, representative during the war of the Brussels Lace Committee, told me that forty communes contributed to her committee, the most important being Syssele (where Valenciennes is the favorite lace), Maldeghem (applications and filet), Saint Andre (Cluny and Valenciennes), Oostcamp and Lophem (Valenciennes), Saint Croix (Cluny and other guipures), and Saint Michele (an unusually beautiful Duchesse de Bruges).

In Bruges itself there are three important convent lace schools, working largely for the shops, but which also execute private commands; the convent school of the Apostolines, typical of those where the children learn a little Flemish, a little French, much catechism, and for the rest make the laces of the region from morning till evening; the school Defoere, and the well-known school Josephine. Each has between 100 and 200 dentellières, who make the popular Torchons and Clunys and Valenciennes, and also the more difficult Binche, with its mesh characterized by the airy *"boules de neige,"* snowballs. They make, too, Old Flanders, which has a particularly strong and elaborate mesh; and of course the Duchesse de Bruges, or Bruges, for which the city is famous. In addition to the convent schools and a few other less important laique schools and some workrooms, one finds in the Hospices, or free homes for the old, another goodly company working together. In their picturesque retreats some 200 old women pass their days making lace, chiefly Valenciennes.

There remain the individual households; to the common statement that in each one, some member makes some kind of lace, one might add, at some time during the year. If the children from these homes do not go to the schools to learn, they are taught by their mothers and grandmothers. A favorite Christmas gift to children is a cushion and set of bobbins, with which they soon learn to produce simple patterns. For example, Madame Roose, the daughter of the concierge of the Groothuis Museum, which houses the marvelous Baron Liedts collection of old laces, accustomed from childhood to see and hear of these laces, became herself a lace-maker and later a successful dealer and now has five daughters of her own, all of whom she has herself taught to ply their bobbins. The Lace Committee told me that during the war the clothing committee had difficulty in finding young girls and women who could darn and sew even moderately well; since childhood they had given all their time to lace-making. Conscious of the danger in this situation, the Lace Normal School preaches that until she has learned other necessary things, no young girl should be allowed to spend more than half a day over her cushion.

By far the greater number working at home make Torchon, Cluny and Valenciennes, tho the Bruges district is celebrated, too, for Rosaline and Binche and Old Flanders, and above all for the Duchesse de Bruges, once so named because it was thought worthy to adorn a Duchess. Bruges lace has always been made entirely with bobbins, in separate flowers, or details that are united not by mesh, but by little picot-edged cords or bars. There are many varieties of this familiar lace; between the

LACE NORMAL SCHOOL, BRUGES, BEGINNER'S CLASS

Symbolic color pattern on left-hand easel; demonstration bobbins attached to colored threads at right

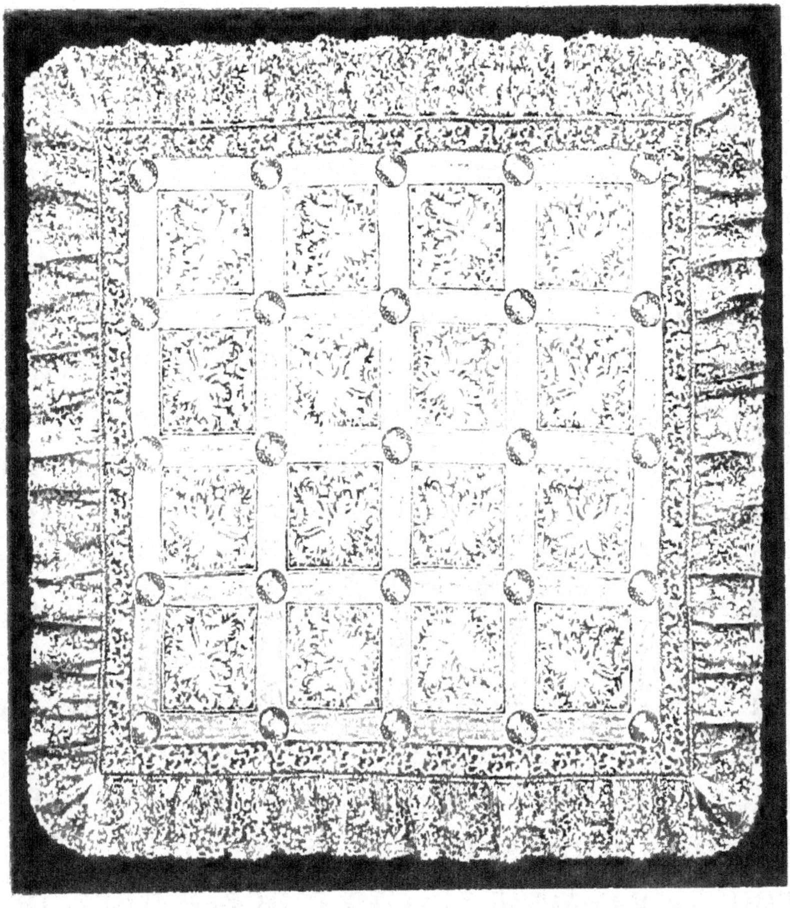

BED COVER IN DUCHESSE, OR BRUSSEL'S LACE

Made with bobbins; executed in Flanders by 30 women in three months; design by The Lace Committee coarse, much marketed modern Bruges, with its well-known roses and trefoils, sometimes scarcely meriting the name of lace, and the Bruges of the robe presented in 1901 to Queen Elizabeth, then the Princess Elizabeth, there is a deplorable distance. The individual trefoils and arabesques and roses of the coarser kinds are made very quickly on the round cushion, which can be readily turned, and are produced in great quantities in many of the communes of the Bruges region, while fortunately in such a village as Saint Michel one can still see exquisite examples of the finer Bruges in the making.

Rather than be introduced to the lace-making of Bruges by the younger workers in the schools, or in one of the thousand homes given over to it, I preferred to go first to the place where probably more strangers, especially English and Americans, have been initiated into the mysteries of the cushion and its bobbins than anywhere else in the world. There have been other famous Béguinages in Belgium—congeries of houses maintained by private endowment, for women, who, while they object to taking the vows of the convent, yet wish to live in a kind of partial retreat from the world and under the protection of the church—but none lovelier than this one of Bruges, with its sixteenth century buildings of pure Flemish architecture, grouped about a wide green court shaded by elm trees. Naturally the Béguinage has not been a mecca for travelers and artists merely because several of the gentle old ladies in retreat there made beautiful lace; they have come in search of its quaint pignons and doorways, its inner gardens, the bridges that span the surrounding canals where the swans paddle peacefully. And they have been delighted to find included in the picture the white-capped women before their lace cushions, intent (doubtless unconsciously) on perpetuating other beauties, as old as those of the buildings encircling the court, the designs of Valenciennes that have been handed down by French and Belgian mothers to their children through generations. These ladies of the Béguinage may keep their private fortunes and pay for the privileges of the retreat. They are supposed, however, to live austerely; their charming brick houses are white inside—wall-papers (as being too gay) are forbidden—while the floors are covered with a kind of pretty, rude rush carpet. They may not go on journeys, and no man outside, except the clergy, may enter the sacred precincts of the court, the gates of which are closed at 8 o'clock. Can one imagine an atmosphere more encouraging to hours spent patiently in lace-making? It is recorded that in the Béguinage of Ghent, in 1756, there were as many as 5,000 women engaged in making the Valenciennes for which that city was famous. But the day of this particular kind of retreat has passed, and even at Bruges many of the houses are vacant; when the old die, there are few who wish to take their places. And it is only because those few who remain preserve the best traditions of the lace that they count in the lace-world of to-day; the quantity produced is negligible. Nevertheless, I was delighted that my first knowledge of Bruges lace should come through the few wide Valenciennes flounces of exquisite flower and vine pattern and firm and even workmanship that I found still pinned to the cushions of the Béguinage.

Curiously enough, in this retreat, pervaded by the sadness that inevitably reigns where the old order changes, I found the young and enthusiastic Vicaire, Professor Maertens, assistant director of the new Lace Normal School of Bruges. He lives with his aunt, who is the mother director of the Béguinage and called "Madame, la Grande Dame," tho she is still Mademoiselle. The Béguinage may in one sense represent the despair of the lace, since what is happening there is happening throughout Belgium. But in the person of Professor Maertens of the Normal School, the Béguinage represents, too, the hope of the lace. In the plain little room of his charming Gothic house, he explained with admirable clarity the necessity which led to the founding of this Normal School by the State in 1911, and the system which it has developed. He then arranged that I should "assist" at the *réouverture* of the school the following morning. There was to be a reopening because, in common with so many schools of Belgium, the Lace Normal had been driven from its quarters by the Germans, and tho after their eviction the teachers had persisted in continuing their classes in a convent, where their persecutors forced them to receive two Austrian pupils (from whom, however, they concealed much), they were in the true sense to begin again on January 7, 1919. That was fully four weeks after the invader had had to evacuate, for eager as they were to commence, with their best effort, they had not been able before this to prepare three school-rooms and a few smaller ones on the ground floor for use. We are accustomed to the pictures of the territories desolated by the Germans, but unless one goes from house to house in the districts supposed to be left unharmed, he can have no conception of the state in which they were left. However, by Thursday morning the few rooms on the ground floor had been disinfected and whitewashed, and the Lace Normal School of Belgium re-opened its doors at 8.30 o'clock. Poets have described the shining faces of children on their way to school—but after pupils and teachers have been ground under the heel of an implacable oppressor for four years there is still another light in their faces as they re-assemble in a free schoolroom. It was generous of them to allow me to share their first morning.

The teachers' course covers two years. In order to insure careful individual training the directors prefer to have no more than eight or ten earnest students in each year's class; they prefer, too, that these shall not have been lace-makers before entering, and that they be between sixteen and thirty years of age. There are, then, two class-rooms, light and airy, and equipped with blackboards and charts, and the all-important large demonstration cushion with its gigantesque bobbins attached to heavy colored wool threads to aid the eye and brain. Each young woman records the steps of her progress in a series of copy-books so beautiful in their penmanship and their drawing as to recall at once the manuscripts of long ago.

What, then, is the instruction which they receive? Since there had never been a system of teaching lace-making in Belgium, the directors of the Normal School were obliged to develop one, and as it exists to-day, logical, comprehensive, far-seeing, it belongs exclusively to the School of Bruges. By the defective method employed before, a pupil was taught to make one kind of lace, then another, and another, but tho she might become proficient in the execution of thirty kinds, she might still be incapable of executing a new thirty-first variety if it were presented to her, because she had not been taught the underlying principles.

The Bruges directors found, after a long and careful analysis of the processes employed in all known laces, that they

ROSALINE, WHICH CLOSELY RESEMBLES BRUGES

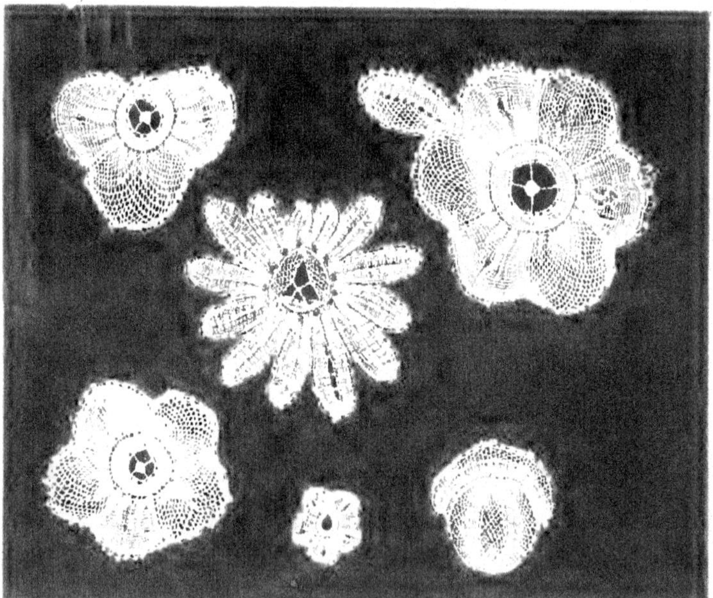

DETAILS FOR BRUGES LACE
Made with bobbins on round cushion

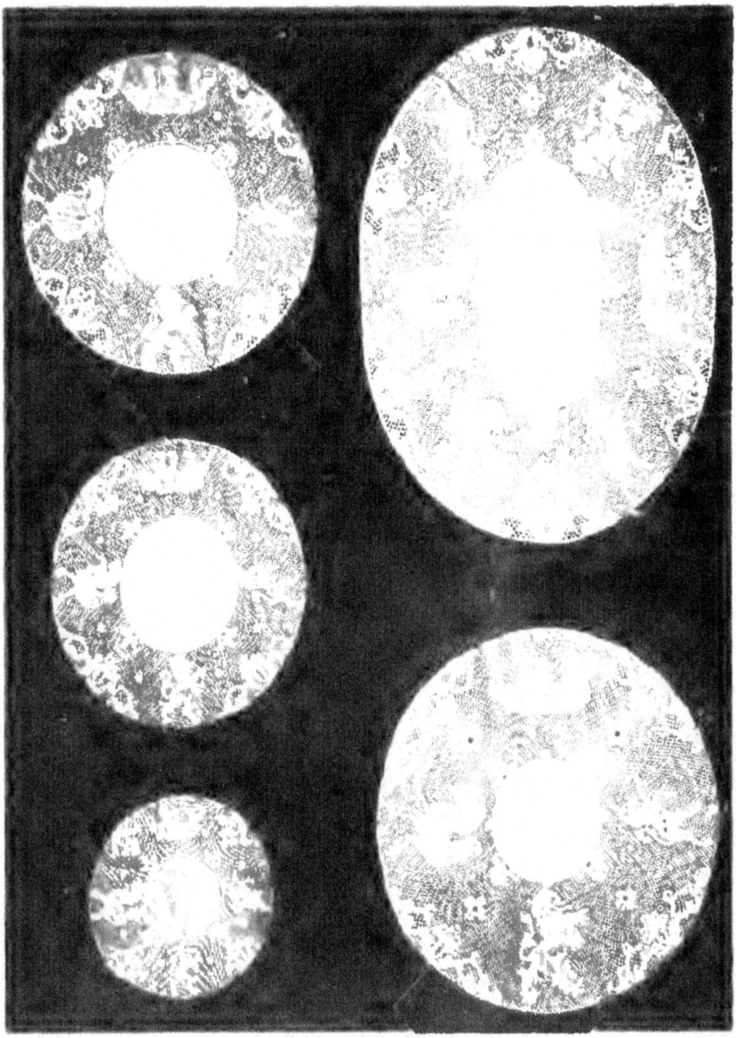

DOILY SET IN POINT DE PARIS IN THE "ANIMALS OF THE ALLIES" DESIGN, EXECUTED AT TURNHOUT depend on but between twenty and thirty major operations, and that, in the final analysis, for the bobbin laces, these reduce themselves always to the simple question, "Does the thread pass from left to right, or does it pass from right to left?"

They chose specific colors, red, purple, green and others, to represent specific movements of the threads, thus establishing a symbolic color system of design which enables the pupil to read a blackboard drawing as he would a written page. And they realized that before the processes are portrayed by lines on the blackboard, they should be executed with the gigantesque bobbins and the colored wool cords.

They then outlined the two years' work, which they made to include classes in practical lace-making, in design, in commerce and English, in the history of lace-making, and religion. Because the two years' course was already over-crowded they did not attempt to teach the needle points, which, according to them, do not demand a system of instruction in the same sense that the bobbin laces require it. Besides, they look upon bobbin lace as more uniquely Belgian and as therefore more necessary to develop. Dr. Rubbens of Zele, farther east, plans soon to have a needle lace Normal School in operation in that town.

In the first year class, a demonstration of the use of the tools, the winding-wheel, the cushion and bobbins is followed at once by the study of the Torchons, which tho they are the commonest known laces, yet in all their varieties employ all the more important lace processes. The Torchons once thoroughly mastered, the student has traveled a considerable distance on the lace journey. The study of Torchon is succeeded by Cluny in all its varieties and Cluny is in turn followed by a kind of barbaric Russian lace, of baroque design, which is, like the Torchons and Clunys, made of linen thread, and resembles them closely in other ways. The finer laces, Valenciennes, Duchesse, Flanders, and others are taught only after these first three groups have been mastered.

Along with the actual lace-making, the students follow courses in design, where they begin first with simple studies in geometry and in drawing. They then execute geometric designs and adapt them to lace-making. From these studies they proceed to drawing from nature, and to what is more difficult, the adaption of the drawings from nature to lace designs, for it is one thing to create a beautiful flower and leaf arabesque, and quite another thing to draw it so that it may be exprest in thread.

The important classes in commerce and English and those in history and religion run parallel with the studies in lace-making and design.

Of great value to these future teachers of Belgium is the model practise school across the court from the main rooms, where at four o'clock each day the poorer children of the neighborhood come to be taught. Each has her cushion and bobbins and pins and thread furnished by the Normal, and enjoys all the advantages offered by its excellent system; while the coming teachers find here the opportunity to perfect their methods.

I asked if these teachers could look confidently to finding positions. Since only the initial class had graduated before the Germans were upon Belgium and since that class was composed almost entirely of women sent from the already existing convent schools, who sought to improve their methods, it is as yet impossible to answer this question. But as this is the single training-school in Belgium (the Brussels School, so capably directed by Mme. Paulis, being chiefly a school of design) there seems to be every reason to hope that once the country has risen from the chaos into which it has been plunged, the Bruges graduates will have no difficulty in securing places. Teachers are as yet very poorly paid, but as regards salaries, too, there is reason to hope. The ideal plan for a school would seem to be that it should be in charge of a graduate of the Normal School, while a specialist in design from the Brussels school should come once a week with her charts and drawings to give particular instruction in that branch. The vital decision as to the part lace-making should have in the curriculum of the communal or free public schools is still in abeyance.

Since factories have killed the lace industry in every other city in Belgium except Bruges and Turnhout, people often ask if it can persist much longer in Bruges. There seems to be good ground to believe it will. Under the Germans the port of Zeebrugge acquired a momentary prominence, but with Antwerp so near, there seems little chance that it will ever become important, or that Bruges herself may look forward to any large industrial development. Lovely, tranquil city guarding a beauty of long ago, it is probable that Bruges will maintain her right to the title "Queen of Lace Cities." "Yes," M. Gillemont de Cock would add, seeing the patterns and quality of the Valenciennes and the modern Old Flanders and Bruges, and Binche, pinned to her cushions to-day, and remembering the exquisite delicate webs of a few decades ago, *"Une Reine, Madame, c'est vrai, mais une Reine bien malade"* —"a Queen, Madame, it is true, but a very sick Queen." The Lace Normal and other schools can help greatly to restore her.

VI

KERXKEN

VI

KERXKEN

Sister Robertine

ON a wet, cheerless day between Christmas and New Year's, I started with Madame de Beughem and Madame Allard for the most important lace district of Eastern Flanders. The Alost region, which in 1896 counted 8,500 workers, is known throughout the lace world for its Needle Point and Venise.

We went first to Alost itself, the center of the area, where, however, modern industries have won their already oft-repeated victory over the lace. It was in Alost, the 16th of November, 1918, that my car had scarcely been able to push its way between the two lines of Belgian soldiers of deliverance holding back the smiling, tearful population, and where, too, I passed Burgomaster Max free after four years in prison in Germany, on his way to King Albert at the Army Headquarters near Ghent.

A short distance south of Alost we passed Haltaert, from which this lace section might more justly take its name, since in Haltaert there is scarcely a household without its needle or bobbin workers. And but a little farther south lay Kerxken, which even in the rain, looked a friendly village and where beside fully three-fourths of the windows women were plying their needles.

Before the war companies of the men of this region went to France to work in the harvest, as many as 40,000 migrating annually, because even before the war, France was short-handed agriculturally and the French fields offered higher wages than their own. The women and girls helped those who remained to gather the crops, and in the fall, when the men came back and the season for working the farms had passed, whole families turned to lace-making as a means of piecing out the gains of the summer. Sometimes the men cared for the children or assisted with the housework so that the women might sit uninterruptedly before their patterns, and in certain instances they themselves made lace—the census of 1896 lists 117 men lace-workers in Belgium. In Kerxken we found that thirty young men who had been silk weavers before the war had during the occupation been able to make lace—not true lace, but such imitations as filet, really a form of embroidery. They made, too, Application, not genuine Application where true lace details, made either with the bobbin or needle, are sewed upon the tulle base, but tulle ornamented with machine-made lacets, narrow braids of various sorts that come to the region from Calais. Lacets usually have a strong thread along one edge, which can be drawn so that the braid may be more swiftly fashioned into curving leaves or flowers. These distressing imitations, which unfortunately pay much better than the true laces, since they can be made with great speed and find a ready market, are a constant menace to them. *"Voilà notre ennemie!"* said Madame Allard, as we looked into a workroom where the table showed little piles of lacet collars. The only method of fighting this enemy is through higher wages for the genuine lace.

We could not see Adele Rulant, once with hardly a peer in Needle Point, to whom people from far and near had sent their old pieces, even shreds of their family treasure, for restoration, knowing that almost certainly her artist's needle would recapture the lost mesh or flower. Adele Rulant had died and we realized again how surely one by one the famous dentellières of the last half of the 19th century are dropping out.

We turned down a lane and were soon at the green door of the convent of the black-robed Franciscaine Sisters, who dismayed, but smiling, hurried forward to greet us, very fresh looking in their white lined coiffes and collars. I say dismayed, because through an error they had expected us the day before and had kept a fire burning for hours, a supreme expression of hospitality in this bitter, coalless winter; this was Saturday afternoon, there was no fire, and the lace-workers were at home scrubbing their tiled floors and doorsteps. But they would light a fire at once, and send a Sister to the nearest houses to recall at least a few of the women; they would prepare lunch for us, a plate of little cakes and a bottle of wine had already been set on the table. Such an apologetic bustle of welcome was heart-warming on a cheerless day. Nothing less, I am certain, would have made it possible for me to drink an entire glass of sour red wine at 10.30 o'clock in the morning.

I wished particularly to visit the convent because I had known during the four years of Sœur Robertine's successive victories over the Germans. After they refused to let laces pass except through their hands, which taxed and had frequently stolen from the parcels, time and again she outwitted them, crossing the forbidden village frontier and carrying the precious rolls herself to the office of the Committee at Brussels.

Beneath the calm of that office there was always tense expectancy; at any moment anything might happen, even the worst thing. One day after weeks of being entirely cut off from many of their lace sections, when the women were more strained and anxious than ever before, the door opened quietly and Sœur Robertine, of Kerxken, a prohibited district, stood before them. Fear for her quite overcame their joy at seeing her; they quickly turned the key and hurried her into a rear room. "But why have you come? We did not send for you—we should never have allowed you to take such risks!"

At first only Sœur Robertine's twinkling, keen gray eyes answered, as she slowly threw off her long black cape and from beneath other garments began unwinding meter upon meter of lovely white lace, till the billowy lengths covered all the table. "It was very simple—I had to come. For weeks our thread has been exhausted; the women are suffering for need of their earnings. I found a way, and I'll find a way back, never fear; we'll all return safely to Kerxken—the thread and the money and I—even tho we may have to slip in under the very nose of the Boche!" She was still laughing and still producing lace, little packets now of square insets and bouquets, when I had to leave.

It was a delight to meet her again here freely directing her convent—she who had so bravely held her right to freedom. Her parents had been shop-keepers and she had brought to the Order a goodly store of practical knowledge and a general alertness and good sense, which added to her unselfishness and swift sympathy and ever-ready laugh, easily explained the admiration and affection generally felt for her.

While we were sitting in the large, cold reception room, waiting for the workers to re-assemble, I asked Sœur Robertine about a painting over the door —a striking portrait which proved to be that of the Curé Van Hoeimessen, who,

POINT DE FLANDRES, OR FLANDERS LACE

Flowers made with bobbins, mesh with the needle; designs by The Lace Committee

HANDKERCHIEF IN NEEDLE-POINT

Made near Alost. Both mesh and flowers made with needle

DETAIL SHOWING SEVEN DIFFERENT FILLING-IN STITCHES

in 1857, founded the convent in an attempt to relieve the misery of the village. A short time before this, greatly distrest by the idleness and poverty of his parishioners, he had asked that a teacher be sent to Kerxken to instruct a few girls in the art of lace-making, and since there was no building in which to start a school, he called the class of five or six girls together in his own house. Then, later, as the experiment succeeded, he invited a group of sisters to come and founded for them the convent of the Franciscaines, which from that day has held unswervingly to the traditions of its foundation in teaching and executing the fine needle laces. There are at present 15 sisters, and about 150 true lace-workers in their lace school. In addition, 300 makers of filet and "imitation" are connected with the convent.

From the salon we went to the workroom, which looks on a deep walled-in garden, a treasure-plot for potatoes and cabbage during the famine years. About a dozen girls and women had dropt their brushes and brooms and hurried through the rain in their wooden shoes to take up their patterns and go on with the delicate traceries of Needle Point and Venise. It was easy to pick out their leader—a beautiful-faced, white-haired woman wearing a black crochet cap, at work on a Venise insertion. She was Sidonie, the best piqueuse, or interpreter of design, in the convent. There were no cushions here, as in the bobbin-lace classes, and the workers held the small, shining, black cloth pattern in their hands, following the pricked holes with their needles; there were fewer of these guiding pin-pricks than in the bobbin-lace picqués. The patterns for Venise and Needle Point are usually small because most women object to large details, as difficult to turn in the hand. Later in a neighboring convent I noticed that the patterns were considerably larger than those at Kerxken, and Sœur Robertine, pointing to them said, "I should have to cut those in two for my girls." Fortunately a detail can usually easily be separated and later rejoined. To protect her lace, the worker covers it with thick blue paper, cutting a hole about the size of a twenty-five-cent piece through which the needle and thread may move freely. Here it was not the marvel of the flying fingers, as in the bobbin-rooms at Turnhout, that most won our admiration, but the skill in directing the fine threads in complicated designs of incredible delicacy. I chose to sit beside fifteen-year-old Colette who held the partly finished section of a handkerchief square beneath her needle. She explained that it was Point de Gaze, gauze point, a name more recently given the old Needle or Brussels Point. And the fragile hexagonal mesh she was weaving between two beautiful full-blown roses, whose raised petals curved outward from elaborately worked centers, seemed most appropriately named. Her cotton, for Needle Point is made with cotton thread, was so fine that I could not, despite her amused reiterations, believe it did not break with every second stitch. A heavier thread had been used to make the flat, closely woven portions of the flowers, and a still heavier one to outline each finished petal or leaf with the *cordonnet* (cord) or *brode,* produced by an extremely firm and regular buttonhole stitch. This cord throws the flowers into very brilliant relief.

Colette had not woven the roses, for because of the difficulty in making it, workers usually specialize on the various individual parts composing this extremely popular lace. A second girl had made the flowers, and a third the exquisite open-work details introduced to lighten

VENISE DESIGNS BY THE BRUSSELS LACE COMMITTEE

HANDKERCHIEF AND JEWEL BOXES, FLANDERS AND VENISE OVER SATIN AND VELVET the whole. Considerable freedom is allowed the lace-worker in the execution of these open-work stitches. If she has talent she may obtain many interesting original results in filling in, for there is apparently no limit to the number of stitches she may employ. In Colette's little handkerchief square, I discovered miniature marguerites and stars and airy balls. Each group had been made by a specialist (many women have spent their lives in making just tiny stars or wheels), and sent to the convent to be bound together with the leaves and roses into a beautiful whole by the clear mesh that dropt hexagon by hexagon from Colette's swift needle.

Colette's neighbor was making the same mesh, but as a background for bobbin-made clusters, sent here from a bobbin-lace village to make the rare Point d'Angleterre, a small quantity of which Kerxken still produces.

In the corner of this class-room were the shelves with the essential skeins of thread; cotton for the Needle Point, linen for the Venise. The linen is more and more difficult to obtain, and since it is hard to handle and breaks easily, has been largely supplanted by cotton thread. There were large cardboard boxes for the drawings and the pricked working patterns; others for the little bobbin-lace roses and leaves and vines that were to be worked into Brussels Point; and still more boxes for the finished meters and insets ready to be sold to the Committee, and later to the dealer who will replace the Committee. While we were examining the boxes a pretty, dark-haired dentellière of about sixteen came in, with work she had finished at home, two handkerchiefs with Brussels Point borders, and two and a half meters of Venise, on which she had worked five and a half months and for which she asked 160 francs, or $40.00.

In the "imitation" room we passed quickly by the lengths of inferior filet and the piles of cheap collars made by men; there was little temptation to linger there. The only defense against that room is more pay for the work across the hall.

We climbed the stairs shivering and looked into the neat little bedrooms with their white board floors, and into the icy chapel where Sœur Robertine declared she could be quite comfortable with only a small black woolen shawl over her shoulders.

We had brought our lunch, but were not allowed to eat it. Sister A., an excellent cook, had prepared hot soup, potatoes and meat, and a dried apple mousse which we persuaded Sœur Robertine to share with us. And after lunch, the orphan and refugee children came in to shake hands, also Janiken, the poor *"idiote"* who is forty-nine years old, but still a child, with a strange, animal-like expression on her face. Sœur Robertine held her hand for us to shake, otherwise little Janiken seemed able to direct her own movements. She smiled and chatted in Flemish, then waddled off quite happy with the candies and cakes we had brought. Janiken spends her days making bead collars and bracelets for the sisters, whom she loves, and when her bead boxes are empty she places them at the foot of the statue at the end of the narrow corridor upstairs, and prays the good Saint Anthony to refill them, that she may weave more necklaces. At night as the sisters pass silently by the statue, they snap the threads of their former gifts, letting the beads shower into the boxes, and in the morning Janiken is happy again.

Sœur Robertine had never ridden in

a motor, and when we proposed that she accompany us to the Franciscaine convent at Erembodeghem, not very far away, her eyes shone. And I shall not forget the faces of the others, as after a further bustle of leave-takings and good wishes, they leaned from the green doorway in the rain, clasping their hands and laughing and nodding, while we tucked their beloved sister into our car. Sœur Robertine herself sat silently and ecstatically in a corner, determined to miss no part of this extraordinary experience.

VII

EREMBODEGHEM

VII

EREMBODEGHEM

The Queen's Cloth

EREMBODEGHEM is a commune of about 6,000 inhabitants, tho the pretty winding street by which we entered, with the picturesque, red-tiled houses clustered irregularly along both sides of it, suggests a smaller village. Nearly all the women in this town, as in Kerxken, make lace, and again it is chiefly Needle Point and Venise. The convent, which furnishes the customary directing and stimulating center, has no superior in the country for its particular laces, unless one grants preference to its own mother house at Opbrakel.

As we entered the courtyard, a group

of French soldiers were warming themselves before a fire they had lighted beneath a dripping canvas tent-roof stretched across a corner of the wall. In the dreary rain the fire flaming against the brick wall, and the horizon blue of the uniforms were a cheery greeting. But inside the convent, alas, there was less cheer; indeed, there was the chill of the tomb, no coal for the poor sisters, who were for lack of it unable to conduct the regular school classes. They told us of their distress over the idleness of the children, who had been turned into the streets by the Germans many weeks before, and whom they were not yet able to reassemble. "Their manners are already so bad," Sister A. said, "that we are ashamed to own them as our pupils." The Germans left the class-rooms in the familiar condition, and the sisters had no sooner finished patching and disinfecting, than the Italian soldiers were billeted there. They were too loyal to criticise but I suspect that their experiences after the departure of the Italians must have convinced them that, after all, a new army is just another army. The French followed, but they at least were occupying only four class-rooms, and the sisters were trying to be optimistic. "We believe they must be better," one of them said, with a smile; "however, we shall not know until they are gone."

"At any rate," she continued, "our lace-room has not been requisitioned; we have had enough coal to keep a little fire there. During all the four years that work has never stopt." Since it was Saturday afternoon there were many vacant chairs in the class-room, but still enough girls were present to enable us to judge of the kind of lace school this is.

Little girls between nine and ten, sitting up very straight in their high-backed chairs, were working with swift, steady fingers and already producing a good Venise insertion of a simple leaf pattern. Several of the other girls were busy with the now well-known Venetian Point medallions representing the arms of the Allied nations, and the provinces of Belgium; still others were executing flower details for yard lace. All this Venise they were making with a needle and single linen thread, for this convent works exclusively with linen thread. They were handling the black cloth patterns, eight to ten inches wide, with apparent ease, turning them with almost every stitch. This mere mastery of the pattern is in itself impressive.

In a corner, near one of the great windows overlooking the walled-in winter garden, a slim, darkly clad girl about sixteen was absorbed in pricking a complicated pattern. Sister A. led me a little aside to explain that this was their feeble-minded girl and that tho they could not

VENISE BANQUET CLOTH PRESENTED BY THE LACE COMMIT

Design by M. de Rudder; executed by the 30

O H.M. QUEEN ELIZABETH ON HER RETURN FROM EXILE
Venise-makers in Belgium in six months

explain it, she was able to interpret correctly very difficult drawings.

At the Committee Bureau I had seen many of the wonderful cloths made from Venise details from this convent (among them the cloth typifying the burning cities, presented to Mrs. Hoover), but I had never imagined anything so lovely as the exhibit the sisters had been arranging on the long, low table, while we were passing from chair to chair following the magic needles. . . . We turned to find the separate parts of a banquet cloth to be offered to Queen Elizabeth on her return from exile, assembled for us. Two hundred and twenty details, there were, on which during the darkest days of the war, women had worked with unfaltering faith and love. M. de Rudder, a well-known Belgian artist, had drawn the design for the Lace Committee. The border, edged with ivy, the symbol of endurance, is composed of ferns and wild flowers, eels and sea-weed, suggesting the forests and fields and waters of Belgium. Adjoining them are the coats of arms of destroyed cities, bordered by a band of lilies of the valley, signifying the return of happiness. In the center, the four patron saints of Brussels, Saints Michel and George, and Saints Elizabeth and Gudule, are enwreathed with olive branches. Saint Elizabeth, above the Red Cross, represents the Queen and her devoted service as nurse during the war, while the eight medallions near her carry the names of the Beatitudes. Opposite Saint Elizabeth is Saint George, who represents King Albert. Below him is the Belgian decoration for bravery, and in the surrounding medallions are woven the names of battles won by him. Between Saint Elizabeth and Saint George, are the immortal words spoken by His Majesty as he went from the Chamber, sword in hand, on the 4th of August, 1914: *"J'ai foi dans nos destinées! Un pays qui se défend s'impose au respect de tous, ce pays ne périt pas!"* It is one thing to mention a few of the two hundred and twenty details of this glorious cloth, it is quite another to hold any one of them in one's hand and realize its perfection, its incredible combination of softness and delicacy and firmness and regularity. The twelve sisters gathered happily about us, as we sat before the table quite breathless over the discovery of one new beauty after another in their truly royal gift.

And then they brought us something much less important, but nevertheless exquisite, the work of Sister S., which they show rarely, a length of Rose Point about four inches wide, and which even the women of the Committee after their long years' constant experience in lace, said they had never seen surpassed. The linen thread ordinarily used in Venise runs from Number 200 to Number 300. This lace, whose base is formed by an ethereal interlacing of vines and tendrils, is made with Number 2000. One can work on it scarcely more than two or three hours a day, and then only under the best light. Sister S. brought me the magnifying-glass, without which I could not have followed the exquisitely varied points, and lifted the infinitesimal petals of the tiny flowers incrusting the background of interwoven tendrils. In some of these microscopic blooms were as many as four layers of petals. It would be useless to attempt to describe the loveliness that results from the blending of the background of vines and lifted blossoms. I asked what a meter of such lace would bring and learned that it will probably be sold in Paris for 1,000 francs, tho these sisters would be happy to guard it as one of their convent treasures.

We had intended going into some of the neighborhood houses to watch the

CUSHION COVER IN VENISE

Pekinese dog design, by M. Allard

TABLE CENTER IN FLANDERS WITH CENTER AND BORDER OF VENISE
Design by Lace Committee; executed in West Flanders by five workers in 15 days

work of the older women, but it seemed impossible to look at any other lace that day and we said good-by. And while the chauffeur brushed away the small boys clinging to or crawling over the car, we again tucked our sister in, to carry her home to Kerxken; it had been a great day for Sœur Robertine and for us.

VIII

OPBRAKEL

VIII

OPBRAKEL

Mother House of a Famous Lace-making Order

AFTER Kerxken and Erembodeghem I was not surprized, when inquiring about needle laces further south, to learn that the only school whose work could dispute first place with them was that of the mother house of the same order at Opbrakel. I had come to know that the finest needle laces of Belgium are made in these convents of the Sœurs Franciscaines.

It was a bitter day, but I determined to reach Opbrakel despite shell-pitted roads and rain. I succeeded even in making a short stop on the way at Cruyshautem Convent, famous, too, for its Needle Point, where the sisters would have detained me longer to describe again and again the entry of the American soldiers at 9 o'clock in the morning on All Saints Day—the wonderful American soldiers who had arrived to free them from their oppressors of four years, and who had remained to buy every scrap of lace in the convent, carrying away the address with the promise to send for more.

In my journeying I discovered a pretty way of learning whose army occupied a particular village—I looked for the first small boy to see which soldier's cap he proudly wore. Thus at Opbrakel, tho it was late afternoon when I arrived, there were children still playing in the street, and the boys jauntily wearing the horizontal blue announced to me that the French were there. These small boys, and later the soldiers themselves, examined my mud-splashed car with much curiosity, as it drew up in front of the convent door.

My visit was quite unannounced, but the sisters held out their hands in welcome, and drew me in out of the rain, speaking, as they did so, words I had almost forgotten, "Hot milk; you must drink a cup of hot milk at once, Madame, and your chauffeur also; this is a cruel day for journeying." They led me to a little room, where I found another unaccustomed comfort, a tiny fire burning brightly. As I sat before it, sipping the sweet milk, the first I had had since leaving America, I remembered the gratitude of travelers in the middle ages toward the convents and abbeys whose doors they found open. The war had brought a return of many of the difficulties and perils that beset them, with the comfortable hostelries of pre-war days pillaged and ruined, the little restaurants or cafés that could do business filled to overflowing with soldiers (I have spent hours in the wind and rain at night vainly trying to find a bed, or a place for my car), with roads wrecked, neither post nor telegraph, nor train, and natural accompaniment of all this disorganization, the necessity of being ever on guard against thieves—in the midst of conditions like these we can appreciate the meaning of the cheering hospitality the convent offers.

While we sat before the fire the Mother Superior had one of the sisters show me a treasure of the school, a framed exhibit, illustrating in miniature all the processes employed in the making of the needle laces, which they had prepared for the last International Exposition at Brussels. Then she recounted for me a little of the history of her lace-making convent, which celebrates its centenary this year, this free year of 1919. I could imagine what it would have meant to try to be joyful over such an anniversary with the enemy heel still on one's back.

One hundred years ago the commune of Opbrakel was in such a wretched state of poverty and misery that among its 2,000 inhabitants, 800 were beggars; and as often happened elsewhere during the period of suffering following the Napoleonic wars, the curé of the commune sought to relieve it by founding a convent which should teach the art of lace-making, to furnish a means of earning bread. He called the Franciscaine Sisters who soon had 100 pupils in their lace-classes, and among them a number of boys. From those days to these, lace-making in this convent has never ceased; there are now not more than 125 pupils in the excellent school, but in the homes of the entire region are those who have learned their art there. The sisters taught first, Chantilly (Opbrakel is very near Grammont, the Belgian home of Chantilly), but about fifty years ago changed from bobbin to needle lace, and since about twelve years ago, they have specialized on the particular needle lace, Venetian Point, in which they are unexcelled. Few of the enraptured tourists in Venise realize that the laces they are buying there were very probably made in Flanders!

Important lace schools and work-rooms have from time to time concentrated all their skill on the production of a masterpiece that might represent them to the world and awaken wide interest and approval. We have a long list of such *chefs-d'œuvres* from the lace-rooms of Belgium, of lovely scarfs and cloths and robes offered to sovereigns or distinguished patrons. And happily during the war the Committee could encourage this practise by giving orders or special "commands" to be executed as gifts for benefactors. Several of these presentation pieces will have enduring value historically as well as artistically.

More than one command fell to the share of Opbrakel, and among others that for a scarf offered to the Queen of Holland in appreciation of her country's generosity to Belgians within Dutch borders. The dentellières, each proud to be selected for the royal task, worked many months on the countless exquisite needle points in this delicate veil. On the scarf ends they united the arms of Holland and Belgium, engarlanding them with hyacinths and tulips, the Dutch national flowers, and about these in turn they wove lilies of the valley, symbolizing the return of happiness. Below the medallion rest the Belgian provinces, enchained, and above them they represented the children of Holland showering flowers of abundance upon the martyred children of their sister kingdom.

It would have been pleasant to talk of other master-works, but we had already sat too long before the fire and we hurried now to reach the large, airy class-room across the court before dark. When starting on my lace journey, I had been warned that, once I had visited the bobbin-lace work-room with all the picturesqueness of the cushion with its mounds of bobbins and clustered pins, and of the flying fingers and the continuous cadences of the clinking wood, I would find needle-lace classes uninteresting. In the beginning this was true; there was nothing particularly dramatic or stirring in a great room filled with girls and young women holding little black paper patterns in their hands and plying a needle above them. But the more I watched these little patterns and the fingers directing the needle and thread, the more marvelous the accomplishment appeared—cotton and linen

"THE TOURNEY" BANQUET CLOTH

Design reproducing a mediæval painting in Tournai, executed in Venise lace by 10 workers in one month, mounting and embroidery by five workers in one month. Price in Brussels, 1,000 francs

ARMS OF YPRES" CUSHION COVER IN VENISE, WITH DETAILS IN FLANDERS so fine that it seemed impossible that any finger should control them—cobwebby, diaphanous meshes, richly petalled tiny flowers, and delicately veined leaves growing beneath just a common needle and a single thread. In the end I looked eagerly for the needle rooms.

And this was the most rewarding one I had yet visited. It happened that the majority of the pupils were busy on the details of a tablecloth recently designed by Madame Allard, in which the linen center is encircled by a family of little beasts as gay as any ever gathered together to cheer a dinner company. I laughed outright, as a little girl, herself laughing, held up an exquisitely worked and most vividly real group of happy ducks floating on a pond. The next showed her enchanting rabbits, another her deer—all along the line they were chuckling over the success of their particular pets. They had captured the sunshine and happy motion of a farm-yard world with just a needle and a single linen thread! Here, as at Erembodeghem, only linen thread is used, because tho it is more difficult to handle, it produces a finer and stronger lace than cotton. After several months (it took six months to execute the first cloth of this design) the details would be assembled and joined by special workers, following the large paper pattern the sisters were now spreading across a table, which had been sent down to Opbrakel from the room of design at Brussels. And the finished cloth, as delightful as an early naive tapestry with its smiling animals, would be sent to the Committee for sale.

Opbrakel stands unquestionably first in Belgium in the production of figures in Point de Venise. During the war, its workers have repeated several times for the Committee their beautiful "Fables de

La Fontaine" series of medallions, as well as those which represent so charmingly "Little Red Riding-Hood," "Puss in Boots," "The Sleeping Beauty," and other much loved fairy-tale figures. These medallions have been sold separately as doilies, or have been combined with Flanders lace or linen in handsome cloths.

It was fast growing dark, and the 125 girls began folding their patterns, and carefully wrapping their delicately pictured little rabbits and ducks to keep them clean till the morrow; maids appeared with dust-pans and brooms, and we gathered up our skirts and stept out into the courtyard. As we crossed it in the dark and the rain it was difficult to refuse the further hospitality of these sisters, who would have kept me for the night.

IX

LIEDEKERKE

IX

LIEDEKERKE

The Last Lace Stronghold of Brabant

IN the court in front of the big brick convent building with its odd little steeple, two sisters, skirts tucked up, and pails swung over their shoulders, Chinese fashion, were about to begin the Saturday scrubbing. Madame Kefer-Mali and I were on our way to Liedekerke, the principal remaining lace center in Brabant, and had stopt in this less important village of Heckelgem for a look at the convent school opened nine years ago.

In the village itself we had found about 150 of the 2,000 inhabitants busy with their needles, for this is distinctly a needle-lace commune, producing a fairly good quality of Venise. Which means that there are as yet no local mills, and tho an adjacent match factory has already attracted a number of Heckelgem girls, most of the women are still content to spend their time making Venise, which they take to the convent, to be sold there to Brussels or other agents.

The convent class-rooms were warm and cheery; fern baskets hung from the ceilings and every window was gay with potted plants. Practically all the village children were gathered inside, and since it was 11 o'clock when we arrived, were happily engaged in drinking their daily Comité National cup of cocoa and in eating the good white biscuit that goes with it. Saturday morning is mending time and on the girls' desks I saw more of those amazing patchwork socks and stockings, the result of three or four

NEEDLE-POINT SCARF EXPRESSING GRATITUDE OF BELC

Executed by 30 w

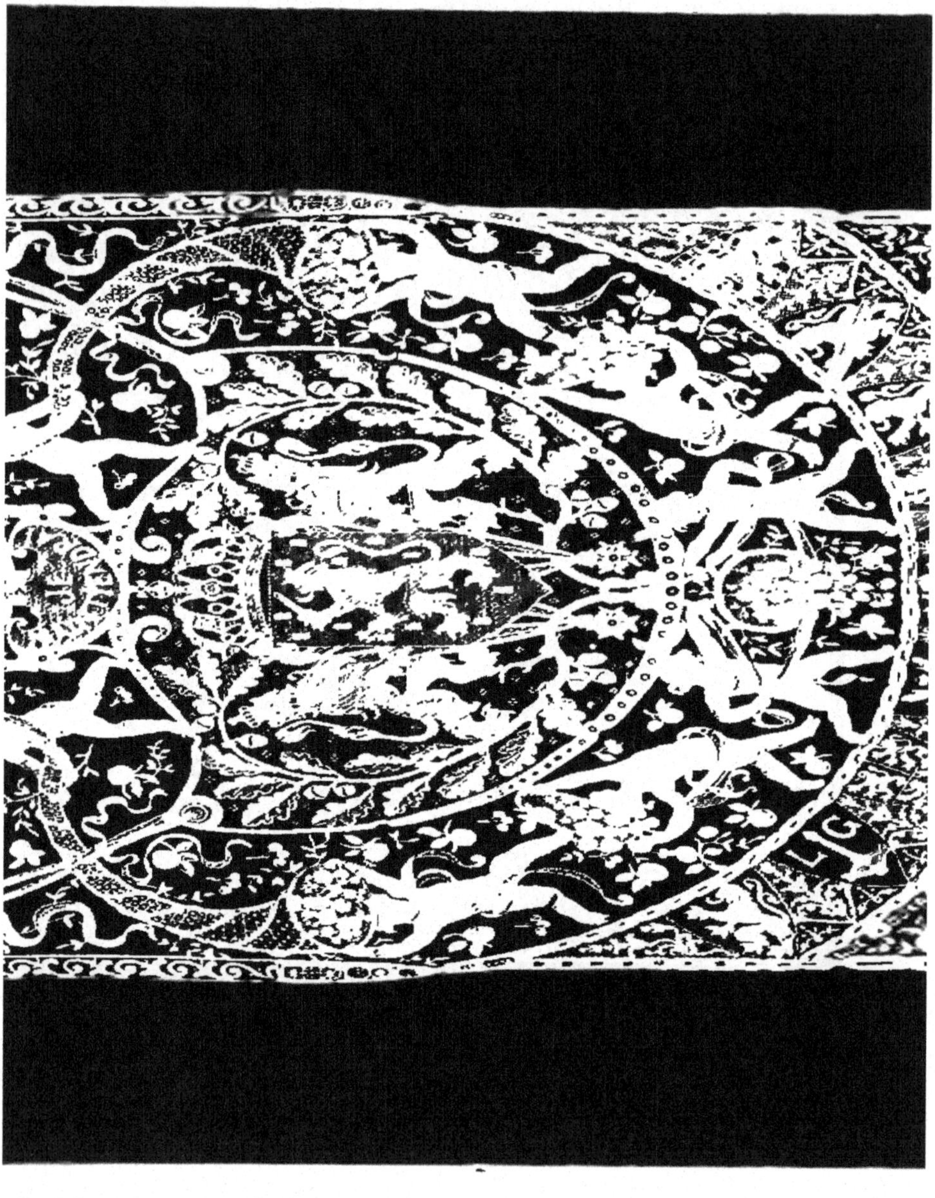

HOLLAND, PRESENTED TO H.M. QUEEN WILHELMINA
n eight months

years' weekly attempts to hold them together.

In the advanced lace class-room, thirty girls, between thirteen and sixteen, were working with cotton thread on Venise insertions and on details for larger pieces. They had come at 8 o'clock that morning, a more humane beginning hour than most schools allow, and would remain as long as there was daylight—looping and weaving with a needle and single thread. I stopt beside Rosalie, who was making a pretty flower detail for a cushion cover. She had begun it five days before and hoped to finish, and receive the seven francs she was allowed for it, that night.

On the table was a pile of chairbacks in Venise, with figure centers and surrounding garlands of flowers all connected by the bars characterizing this lace—an order for a Brussels dealer, who had recently offered fifty-two francs each for them. The sisters were excited and happy over this new price, which was considerably more than anything Heckelgem has hitherto been able to command, one and a half francs a day having been the average wage of the best workers.

A little farther to the south and still in Brabant, tho it lies near the Flanders border, is the much better known convent of Liedekerke, which boasts an unbroken record of sixty years of lace-making, and which before the war received a yearly subsidy of 800 francs from the "Amies de la Dentelle." As we walked beside the pretty orchard and vegetable garden, bright with purple cabbages, that form the entrance court, toward the rather impressive red-brick buildings, again with their odd miniature steeple, I saw the great arms of a Dutch windmill turning lazily somewhere in the rear. And nearer the door, off at the left in a side court, a war-kitchen with tiled floor and uncertain roof, where hundreds of the village poor still were coming for their daily pint of soup. Of the 4,000 inhabitants as many as 2,900 were forced on to the soup-line during the occupation.

This, then, was one of the important and successful convent schools of Belgium; but in January, 1919, it was in a much sadder plight than the little neighboring school at Heckelgem. There was no coal, not a class was in session, not a child at work with her bobbins. At 4 o'clock in the afternoon, on Monday, October 28, when there were between 800 and 900 children, among them 100 lace-workers, gathered in the various classrooms, German officers had appeared to announce that by 7 o'clock the rooms must be cleared of both teachers and children. I had already had many demonstrations of what taking possession of school-rooms meant. It was not necessary that the sisters should lead me from room to room, pointing out this or that ruined wall, or casement torn away, or vacant space where the benches or chairs burned as firewood, once stood; but I followed them about for their own sakes. There was at least a kind of comfort in being able to furnish proof of these outrages to somebody.

One small room was undisturbed, but it was a sadder room than any of the others. The primary lace-class had occupied it, and several rows of little girls were learning to make their first flowers and leaves when the enemy drove them out. The baby chairs and the cushions were just as they left them, tho thick dust dulled the blue of the linen covers and the tiny unfinished white roses and tendrils held by the rusty pins. One would have liked to bring the enemy mothers into this room with its baby chairs, and its dust-covered unfinished roses.

In the large adjoining hall Sister M.

kindly came to work at a table, on Application, one of the laces for which Liedekerke has been especially distinguished. Before the English invention, early in 1800, of machine-made tulle, which had an incalculable influence on the development of the lace-industry, all meshes had to be made either with the needle or with bobbins. The factory substitute for these difficult processes won instant favor, and with the general public the more swiftly made and cheaper tulle Application, supplanted the exquisite Point d'Angleterre, which it imitated. Liedekerke, for example, had begun its lace career with Point d'Angleterre, and in changing later to Application, was merely responding to popular demand. Its sixty years of lace-history reads: Point d'Angleterre, Application, Rosaline.

These things Madame Kefer-Mali explained, as Sister M. was placing her square of blue paper on the linen of the table cushion, and then the bobbin-made bouquet, wrong side up on the blue square, pinning it carefully and smoothly through the paper to the cushion. Over this she stretched her scarf length of tulle. I was surprized at the time and painstaking effort she gave to these simple operations, until I saw later the effect of the slightest carelessness on the finished flounce. Almost any clever needlewoman can join a flower to a piece of tulle—but only an artist can produce a beautiful scarf or veil in Application. Once the bouquet was properly placed and pinned, Sister M. began to sew, lifting the tulle lightly with each stitch, and smoothly attaching all the edges, for this bouquet was being appliquéd on the body of the scarf. Had it formed the border one edge would have remained free.

Liedekerke Convent, to which some 200 of the villagers bring their laces and which once made little else than Application (many beautiful robes and flounces and scarfs have gone out from the commune and the school), now makes comparatively little of it; for during the last six years Paris and other markets have asked for Rosaline. It is to be hoped that this small quantity may be continued, and that the lace world may still win at least a few pieces yearly of the earlier, more exquisite Point d'Angleterre.

Point d'Angleterre, so named because of its great popularity in England, reached its height in beauty and in favor during the seventeenth century, when it occupied the talent and energy of all the lace-workers of Brussels. It differs from Needle Point, in which both flowers and mesh are made with the needle. It is one of the loveliest of all laces, combining in rare beauty, rich bouquets and arabesques and birds of finest bobbin work, with a frail transparent needle mesh, the flowers themselves becoming frequently more light and delicate through the introduction of charmingly varied needle-worked open spaces. Certain workers make the flowers, and others the connecting mesh. If one can imagine the softness of a kind of sublimated or diaphanous velvet, added to the fragility of an airy and cobwebby lace, one may have some idea of the effect of good Point d'Angleterre. And if one would possess a collar or a flounce, one should buy it quickly, for Point d'Angleterre is going the way of the other difficult and exquisite points. Such villages as Kerxken, Liedekerke, Destelbergen (near Ghent), and those of the Alost region still make occasional pieces.

The more ordinary Point de Flandres, or Flanders, so generally produced to-day, has the same composition as Point d'Angleterre, since in it bobbin-work flowers are joined by a needle-mesh. And even tho coarser and less complicated

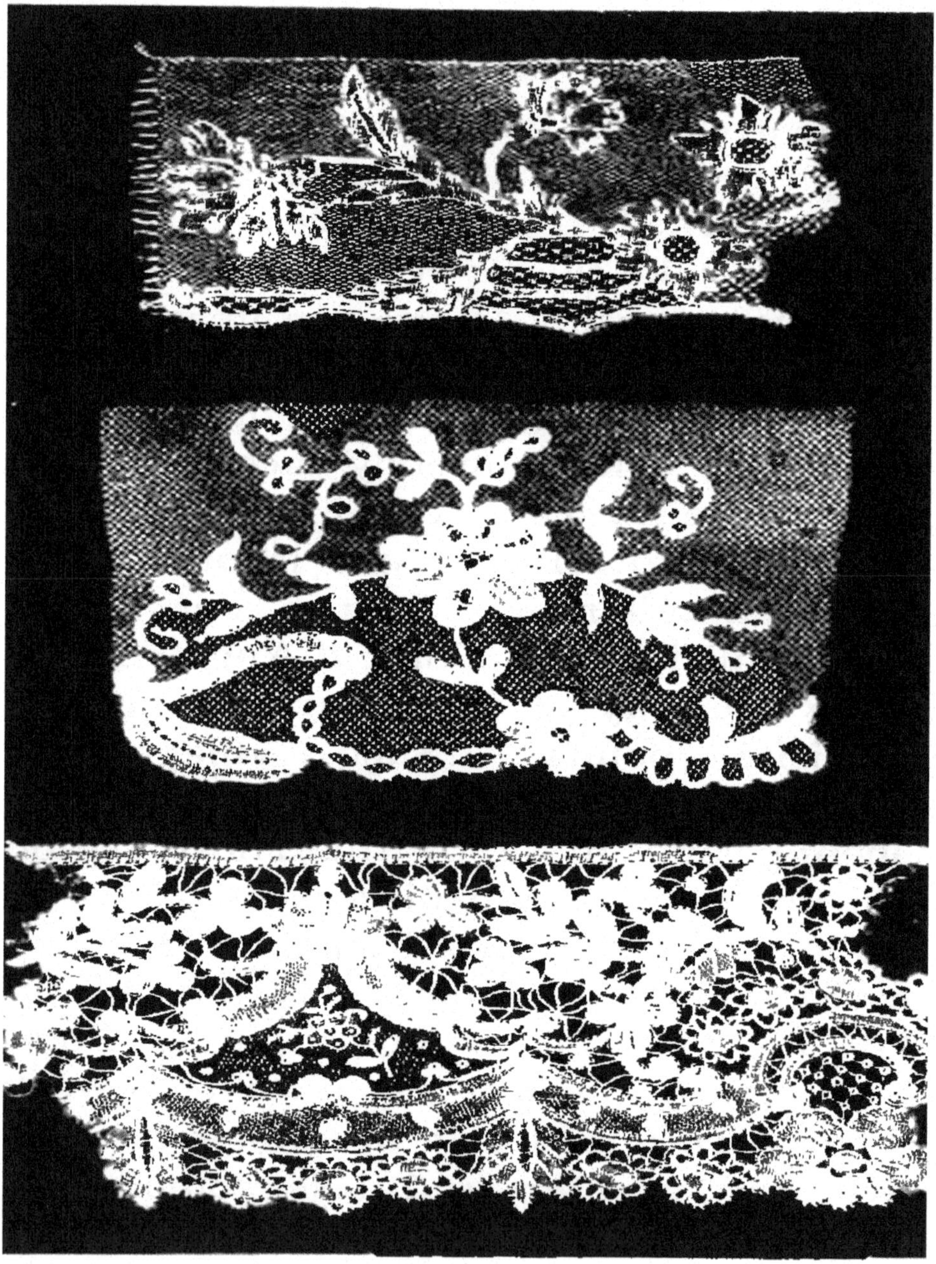

BOBBIN LACES
(1) Malines. (2) Application, flowers sewn on tulle
(3) Duchesse, with needle-point insertions

APPLICATION DETAILS TO BE SEWED ON TULLE

Upper flower shows open spaces left by bobbin worker for needle worker; lower flower shows both bobbin and needle work completed than Point d'Angleterre, Point de Flandres is also difficult to make, and should be much better paid. There are innumerable differences in quality, and many ways in which this lace may be employed. The Committee has used it chiefly in elegant table centers and cloths, in lamp-shades and in various articles to embellish a drawing- or dining-room. And this summer of 1919 it is being used with much success by important French houses as trimming for dainty *ninon* underclothing. Nineteenth century Point de Flandres, then, is little more than a commercial name for a very coarse kind of Point d'Angleterre.

This Point de Flandres must not be confused with Old Flanders or Antik, the ancient bobbin-lace experiencing a happy revival at present. Old Flanders is, like Cluny, made entirely with bobbins and with uncut threads; in other words, in single lengths, and not in separate or cut details.

Liedekerke, then, first made Point d'Angleterre for which, after a certain time, it substituted Application, changing again about two years before the war to Rosaline, suddenly become a popular lace.

Rosaline is not very different in appearance from the finer varieties of Bruges; in fact, it employs much the same technique, and is made as is Bruges with bobbins, in small pieces, which are later joined by special workers. A dentellière who can make fine Bruges can usually make Rosaline. Each small piece is composed of elaborately interlacing flowers and leaves and arabesques, without a connecting mesh, but joined by *brides* or bars, with a picot edge. Sometimes the tiny incrustations called pearls, common to Burano lace, are added, to further ornament the richly covered ground.

I watched a Rosaline cushion, on which the pattern of an arabesque detail was pinned, and Sister A., as she began to shift in pairs the fourteen bobbins needed to execute it; one pair, the *voyageurs,* were continually traveling from right to left and back again as she wove the flat parts of the leaves and blossoms. The Rosaline technique is particularly difficult, since the pins must be continually and rapidly changed as the worker, with a crochet-hook, lifts the thread to pass her bobbin through in the characteristic loop stitch. This delicate operation, constantly repeated, strains both eyes and nerves. The pins are placed along the outside edge of the flowers, instead of inside, as in Bruges, which produces the picot or looped-edge effect of Rosaline. In Bruges the flower edges are even.

I turned from the arabesques just beginning to grow on the cushion, to a lovely little finished detail, about four inches square, one of several in a box which was to hold them till they could be joined to make a scarf. It had taken seven days of thirteen hours each to make this four by four piece, which meant that the maximum a skilled worker could earn in executing it was about two francs a day.

The Liedekerke convent school does not accept children under twelve for more than two complete afternoons a week and for more than one hour each of the other days, these hours being lengthened gradually until the girl of sixteen gives her entire time to her lace. The sisters hope that once they find coal and thread and can put their class-room in order, they may again have 100 pupils, and that the village may continue to count at least 200 good dentellières.

X

HERZELE

X

HERZELE

A Château of Refuge

THERE are certain châteaux in Belgium that will be remembered throughout this century as harbors of refuge; they dared not flare beacons from their roofs, but during four dark years, people of the nearby communes knew that day and night lights burned there for them. The château of the Comte du Parc was such a one, a property lying on the edge of the village of Herzele, south of Alost, which, tho the house itself is unpretentious, embraces a lovely park and wood, and from which, incidentally, the Germans cut 1,000 trees.

It is no longer only the estate of the du Parcs, it is the loved shelter of every villager accustomed to hurry toward it in sad or perilous hours. The morale of the entire region was sustained by the knowledge that the people of the château had not left, as they easily might have, for their safer Brussels home, in the zone of civil administration, where if not free, they would at least have been less imprisoned, but had chosen to remain in the military zone, utterly cut off from their relatives and the rest of Belgium.

They might have considered several reasons sufficiently important to call them away (the Bourgmestre of Herzele had found at least one, his ill-health); among other things their château was as yet practically uninhabitable. It had been begun only a short time before the war broke out, and with the sounding of the first alarm the workmen had rushed out to report to their officers, leaving electric cords dangling, unmounted fixtures standing against the walls, and neither hot water nor heating systems installed. Madame told me later of her desperate and amusing efforts to fasten locks on the most important doors. As she and her husband were debating how they might arrange one large room in the left wing as their single general living-room they could already see the villagers coming anxiously along the tree-lined avenue and across the park to inquire if they were still there. "After the first troubled questions," Monsieur said, "even if we had not already decided we must stay, it would have been quite impossible to go away."

The soldiers of the village were leaving with scarcely time for good-bys; Madame understood the fears of the women who came to the château for comfort; her only son, too, a brave, handsome boy, was off to join the colors—her brave, handsome boy, who now lies buried not far from the Yser.

In October the victorious Germans pushed southward, and from the 14th to the 18th, shrapnel fell like rain on the park, but the château escaped unharmed. Then three officers of the occupying army rode up on horseback, revolvers in hand, demanding that the Comte present himself immediately. Madame followed her husband, not knowing what to expect. To their first threat, Monsieur replied calmly, "I do not like those objects," and after a moment's hesitation the officers lowered their weapons. Then they demanded guaranties that they would be absolutely safe from attack by any person, either of the château or the village. "I can, of course, speak for my château," Monsieur answered, "but I can not be responsible for the villagers if they are pushed too far." These villagers themselves told me later that they were convinced it was only the presence of the Comte (the bullies were frequently servile before titles and powerless before fearlessness) that saved Herzele from destruction. "We always expected the worst," they said; "in the early days, when the Boches lighted a great fire in the wood, we rushed to the château, believing it was burning."

From the beginning, Madame and her two daughters looked for some constructive aid they might give their women, something more than the general relief furnished by the Comité National.

Of the 2,500 inhabitants of the village, 1,700 were soon on the lists of the helpless or destitute; among these were many tuberculosis victims. The château living-room became first a clothing bureau, where daily all sorts of garments, sent from America, were distributed. Madame engaged some of the women of the village to patch and re-fashion these, and with certain sums of money that succeeded in reaching her from time to time from an American lady who had "adopted" Herzele, she was able to purchase new materials and offer further saving employment. I do not know the American lady, but if she could have seen Madame's eyes as she told me of what it meant, imprisoned as they were, to receive these gifts from some one outside who remembered them, I do not doubt she would have felt sufficiently rewarded.

In 1916, when I was in Belgium as a member of the Commission for Relief in Belgium, the Germans prevented my going near Herzele, or any point in the zone of direct military preparation, so I could follow the work of Monsieur and Madame only through the Brussels Lace Committee, which had itself great difficulty in keeping connected with them. They made their judgments from the ever increasing quantities and improved quality of the laces that somehow came through.

The room in the château was the lace office not only for Herzele, but for eleven additional villages, where between 2,500 and 3,000 girls and women, encouraged by the Committee support—its designs and thread and money—were busy with their needles and bobbins; for while this is chiefly a needle-work district, large quantities of bobbin laces are also made. To be sure, none of these laces is superior, but they are good, and marketable. They include Cluny, Duchesse de Bruxelles, a kind of coarse Flanders (where the flowers are made with bobbins and the mesh with the needle), Venise, and Rosaline; and of these the Flanders and Venise are most important. At times it was not difficult for the dentellières to take or send their finished lace to the château, at others they were threatened with fines and imprisonment if they were discovered trying to get it there. To refer to but one instance, the facteur of the village three miles distant was fined seventy-five francs when caught on the way with his pieces. The Germans were doing their utmost always, to attach lace-makers to their *Spitzen Centrale,* and despite the international agreement which engaged their protection of the work of the Brussels Lace Committee, they interfered with and obstructed its work again and again. At one point they insisted that all deliveries to the Committee should be made through them, and that they be paid 1 per cent. on the value, in gold, for transmission, where transmission, unfortunately, only too often spelled for them retention.

In the village Madame and her daughters went from house to house, instructing and comforting. The days of the deportations were more terrible than any others. In remembering that first hideous deportation night in Herzele, one remembers, too, that early in the war Cardinal Mercier said that while there was once a time, when to make people believe, we felt we must heighten, or embellish the cold facts, that now in order that they should believe, we must withhold part of the truth. That first night, men and boys were torn from their beds and herded into the school, from there to be carried off in cattle-cars to Germany. There was neither light nor heat, and in the cold and the darkness, the tortured little village broke into a great cry of lamentation, while the château was filled with wives and mothers seeking comfort.

Later, when the activist troubles became acute, the two daughters held meetings even in the cabarets to urge loyalty to a united Belgium. They believe that not one person in their entire village can be said to have worked for the enemy, except when deported bodily, or otherwise coerced.

Somehow the years passed, and then one day, the 16th of September, 1917, bits of white paper fell like snow from the clouds. The family rushed out to gather them and found Lord Northcliffe's celebrated posters, "The First Million," representing a vast multitude on the march, the statue of liberty in the background, the fields of France in the foreground, and a continuous bridge of ships connecting them. This snowfall was followed by others, and each brought hope.

Finally, in October, 1918, the Germans, knowing the Allied Army of Liberation was almost upon them, again pulled their guns up into the château grounds, but in the final fighting, as in the earliest, the house somehow escaped.

When I reached Herzele, in January, 1919, the wide park was beautiful and still, green things were sprouting beneath the trees, there were a few birds; to a stranger there was little evidence of the terrible years. But inside, in the cold, unfinished hall, the electric cords still dangled; everything was as the Belgian workmen had left it four and a half years before. And in the single living-room at the left, rudely furnished, but including through large windows the beauty of the park, there were still the war-time desk and long table with the piles of trousers and shirts at one end, and the rolls of white lace at the other. I shook out a scarf of Duchesse de Bruxelles of flower and leaf pattern, with insets in needle work, and several wide flounces of Flanders lace, of the same pattern I had seen used in the charming lamp-shades on sale in the Committee room at Brussels. There were also rolls of Bruges, and Rosaline, Application, and Point d'Angleterre.

As I examined them, Monsieur got out his records and discust the future of his lace-workers. "I am convinced they will be happy to continue in this district, if only they can be sure of a living wage. And apart from other determining factors, to make that, they must learn to execute laces of better quality. We need, above all, a school which will offer along with its courses in practical lace-making, training in design. During the war we had many beautiful designs from the Committee, but each time we were cut off from them we realized our helplessness. In one of the villages the patterns are drawn by a furniture-maker. One reason for the wretched condition of the workers before the war was their entire dependence on the particular lace dealer who furnished them their patterns and their thread, and who, of course, protected his models by copyright. The old, unprotected designs, which may be copied by any one, are little in demand, and during the process of generations of re-copying, many of them have so greatly deteriorated as to become scarcely recognizable. If our women were trained they could restore these, and, what is more important, some of them, at least, could invent new ones."

I asked what it would cost to found a school and support it during its first year. "Perhaps 20,000 or 25,000 francs; we might hope that the State would undertake such a work, but with its present overwhelming burden, it is a question if the Government can occupy itself with lace needs. If it could be started by private initiative, and prove successful, I believe there is no doubt that the Government would be willing later to subsidize it."

Madame brought a picture post-card from the mantel, of three brothers who had been deported, two of whom had not returned. Other men were drifting back from Metz, where most of the *déportés* from Herzele had been for over two and a half years, but these two would not return, for they had been frozen to death. I understood at once, for I remembered the sixty-five men with black arms and legs who had been "returned" to the Brussels Hospital in 1917. "No"; Madame looked at the portrait of her boy, with the Belgian colors above it and a vase of flowers in front, and then again at the little post-card; "No," she said simply, "I have no desire yet to go to Brussels. I prefer to remain here with my people, where we may still, from time to time, weep together."

XI

GHENT

XI

GHENT

A Lace Queen of Long Ago

OF the cities I visited during three months' continuous travel in Belgium following the armistice, Ghent appeared to me to be attacking her problems with greatest speed and vigor. Brave old Burgher city of canals and mellow buildings and bell-towers, this Flemish capital is at the same time an active, modern, commercial center; which explains why Bruges has been able to win from her the title she once proudly held of "Queen of Lace Cities."

The lace history of Ghent begins with the lace history of Belgium, in the sixteenth century; but her great period dates from the seventeenth century and the introduction of the epoch-making mesh of Valenciennes. The activity of her women and girls, following the appearance of this new lace, surpassed anything she had hitherto known; it was not long before the music of 1,000,000 bobbins rose to meet the riotous pealing of her bells. In the sixteenth century Malines had undisputed first place in lace; Ghent now outstript her. One wonders if part of the fascination of this city for the men the United States sent there in 1814, to make peace with England, and who, after six months' lingering, had to be urged to return home, lay in its clicking bobbins and the joyous garlands that blossomed under them.

There is a portrait in the Hôtel de Ville, where one may see the Empress Marie-Thérèse, wearing the marvelous Valenciennes and the Needle Point robe presented to her by the Canton de Gand in 1743. And scarcely more than a century later, in 1853, the city made its last gift of similar magnificence—another robe, valued at 20,000 francs, on which 80,000 bobbins were employed unceasingly during six months, and this time offered to the Duchess of Brabant, Marie-Henriette. There were no succeeding world-stirring gifts of lace because Ghent had begun to think of other things, of industrial and commercial development, and as she advanced in these, the art of lace-making declined, until to-day it has ceased to exist.

However, in the surrounding communes (the region counts fifty) there are still perhaps 2,000 dentellières making most of the bobbin and needle varieties, the best among them being Valenciennes, Flanders, Duchesse, Needle Point, Bruges and Rosaline. The Comtesse de Bousies, chairman of the Ghent Lace Committee during the war, did her best to encourage the work in these outlying districts, and was able to help, in addition, many needy women in the city itself.

In 1917, for instance, Celine appeared at the office to ask for thread. She was twenty years old, and before the war had been one of the 10,000 women employed in the linen spinning mills; her mother was ill with tuberculosis, her father without work, and also ill; there were five younger children. "I know I have not proper fingers," she said, as she held out her rough hands, "but if you will only promise I may bring my lace, I believe I can learn." The Committee believed this, too, and because she worked with intelligence and with almost feverish eagerness, she was soon assured the minimum wage of three francs a week, and later the larger sums made possible with the Committee's success. Shortly before the armistice, the mother died, and only last week Celine came again to the desk to ask anxiously if the Committee could not somehow arrange, that even after they had disbanded, she might continue to make lace. Her father had found a little work; she wanted to remain at home where she might at least direct the younger children, and she could, if only she were sure of her war-time wage. Could not the Committee promise the sale of her laces? Often repeated question during these courage-testing days, when emergency organizations are breaking up, and poor women do not yet see what is to replace them.

Among the more important communes on the Ghent committee list, I found Oosterzele, Baelegem, and Landsanter, all three producing a good quality of Duchesse, Flanders, Needle Point and Venise, and counting together about 160 lace-makers; Gysenzeele and Destelbergen, which make fine Flanders, and Duchesse, Knesselars, with 250 Cluny workers; Asper with 60 in Venise; the convents of Scheldewinkle and Eecke, the first occupied with Venise, the second with Needle Point and Duchesse, which it sells to an American house, and finally, the larger Deynze district, including Vynck, Lootenhulle, Machelin, the Valenciennes convent school at Ruysselede, and Bachte, with perhaps 400 lace-makers in all.

I got my orientation for this last southern district from the Comtesse d'Alcantara, who has been indefatigable in her double rôle of chairman of Deynze and vice-chairman of the regional committee. Constantly throughout the war, she might have been seen starting from the handsome château at Bachte—one of the most imposing in Belgium—on bicycle or on foot on her way to one of the lace villages, with thread and money for the workers, or at night returning with the rolls of lace which she had then to get to

Ghent and from there to Brussels. The Germans never succeeded in obstructing her work, nor that of her father and mother, for their villagers and for the orphans of the entire region. Women came between shells to bring laces. It was a moral help just to be able to talk about their work.

As I crossed the moat and passed under the archway, I saw the spot where the last Allied shell exploded, killing nineteen Germans, while the family and the 200 villagers in the cellars, where they had been for two weeks, escaped unharmed. In fact, in all the Deynze country I was in the midst of the destruction accompanying the final push of the liberating army, and was vividly reminded of what would have happened to the rest of Belgium had the armistice been further delayed.

But already in the partially wrecked villages many of the women had gone back to their cushions — their reason-saving cushions, for they furnished practically the only employment to be had, and however small the earnings, they at least insured a few francs a week, and best of all they proved that something of the past persisted.

In Vynck, a poor little town of 1,700 people, I found 40 Valenciennes-makers, and heard that 100 young girls were being taught at home by their mothers. I talked with two maiden sisters—one 68, the other 72—whom I spied hidden behind a window-screen of potted plants, working, with 450 bobbins each, on a kind of Valenciennes one finds only on the cushions of the past generation. They could not repeat often enough their gratitude to the Committee, which had been paying them 44 francs ($8.80) a meter for their lace, so much more than they had received before the war from the Courtrai facteur to whom they had sold.

They counted on making about five meters during the winter ($44 worth), and they work from dawn sometimes till nine at night.

In a neighboring house was a grandmother of eighty-one and her granddaughter, and on the grandmother's cushion such a covering and re-covering of bobbins and lace, to keep them spotless. Over all she had spread a large towel, beneath it a worn napkin, then a piece of pink gingham, and below that two remnants of white and blue cloth, and it seemed appropriate that the snowy treasure, Valenciennes, too, should be revealed to me only after such a ceremony of unveiling as this bent old woman of Vynck performed.

I passed quickly through Lootenhulle with its 125 workers, who make, among other varieties, good Duchesse and Rosaline; and Hansbeek, which produces a superior Valenciennes; and Ruysselede, with its excellent school for Valenciennes; to cross from the south to Destelbergen, which lies almost directly east of Ghent. All the plain was white under the first deep snow of winter, but to enjoy its loveliness one had to be able to forget the torn roofs and fireless hearths.

At Destelbergen I went at once to the atelier of Mme. Coppens, to whom women of both France and Belgium send their old Applications and spider-web meshes, for restoration. Before the war she employed seventy expert lace-makers in her school, now she can depend on no more than twenty—tho there are some 100 less skilful ones in the village. On this particular January day the school was empty. As Mme. Coppens received me, she said, "I regret, Madame, but I am without coal, and without thread; I have been forced to close my work-room; however," she hesitated an instant, "if Madame does not object to coming into

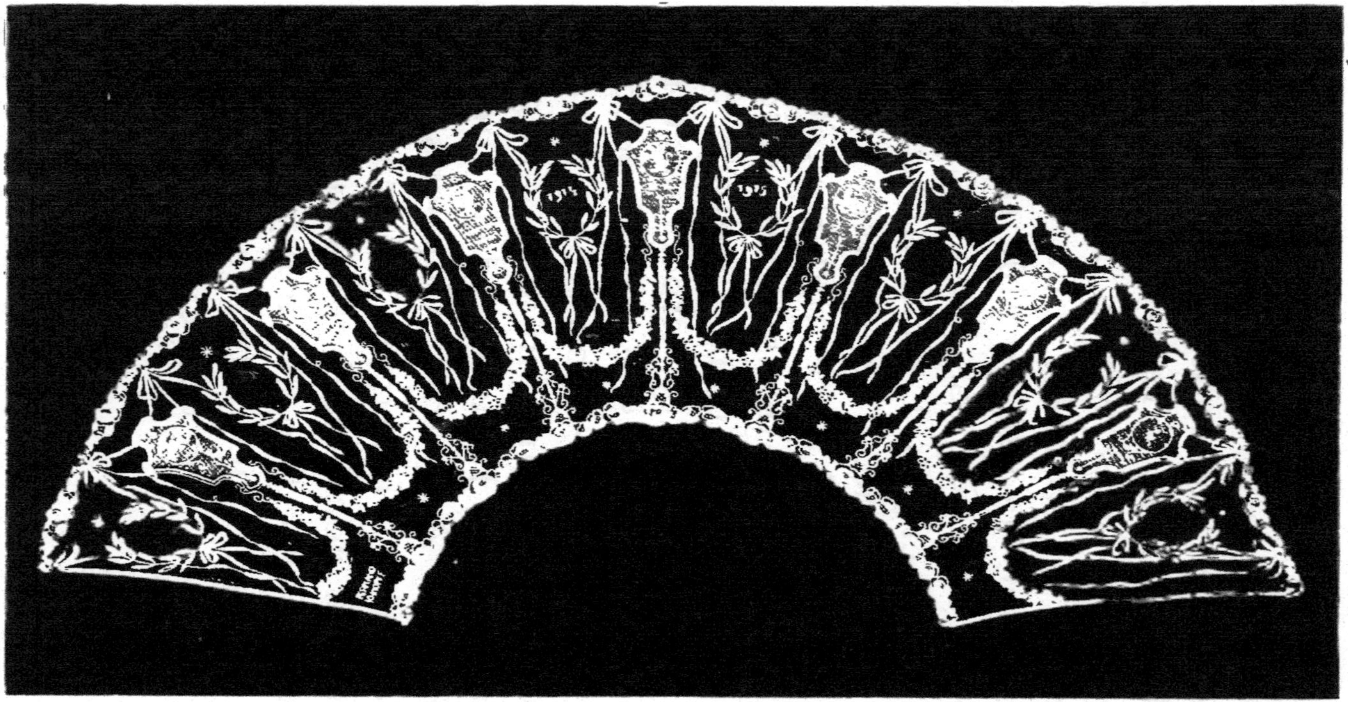

FAN IN NEEDLE-POINT

Executed by three women in six weeks. "Shields of the Allies," design drawn by M. Knoff for the Lace Committee

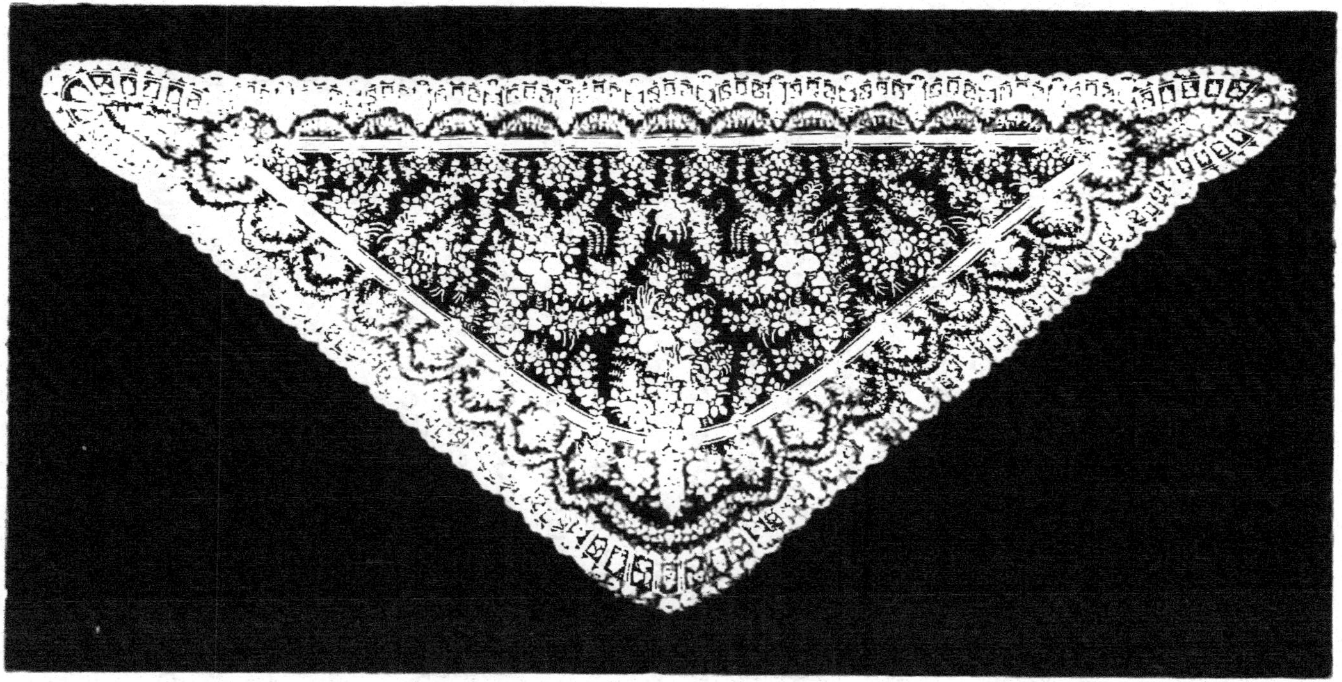

EIGHTEENTH CENTURY MARRIAGE VEIL IN NEEDLE-POINT, BELONGING TO COMTESSE ELIZABETH D'OULTREMONT

It would take 40 workers about a half year to copy this veil the kitchen, she may yet see Stéphanie, the first lace-maker of the village, at work."

Remembering the glistening shelves and floors of other Flemish kitchens, I did not mind; happily not, for in the end Stéphanie was more to me than many villages. She was bending over an immaculate cushion, seventy-eight and unmarried, and all her person as scrupulously neat as her cushion, from her odd little peaked black crochet cap to the felt shoes she had made herself. She was weaving the flat surfaces of a dainty French bouquet, and as I stept toward her chair, looked up, delighted that some one was interested in what she was making. When I picked up a Bruges collar on the nearby table she tried in ejaculatory Flemish to make me understand, that even tho she had made parts of it, she disowned the whole as unworthy the name of lace, and she brought my eyes back to the delicate texture of the leaves and petals on her cushion.

I wished to know what Stéphanie was getting for a day's work on her fine bouquets. She has been making lace for seventy years, is intelligent and quick, and her maximum wage is two cents an hour, a franc for a day of ten hours. I asked about the future—she has thought of that, not without anxiety, and is providing at seventy-eight for what she calls "old age" by trying hard to put by two cents a week. Madame C. has been kind to her, and gives her as much freedom and comfort as she can offer; for instance, when Stéphanie was ill for three days last week, she did not deduct her wages. She would gladly double her pay, or triple it, for she realizes there are few like Stéphanie left, but the Paris firm to whom she sells pays so little for her lace that she has never been able to offer more than a franc a day. "If I could give two francs, I could quickly gather a company of 1,000 contented lace-makers, I am certain," she said. "But when my old workers fall ill or die, I find no young girls willing to come to me; they prefer the twenty francs a week they can make picking wool. When Stéphanie goes, I shall have no single artist to replace her. *"C'est un vrai cœur de dentelle"* (she is a true heart of lace), she said affectionately, as she patted her on the shoulder.

And then she went to fetch a cardboard box and I took a chair by the table, to watch her unfold what it might contain. She spread three beautiful widths of Application on blue paper so that I might better see the tiny bouquets and scattered buds and leaves that blossomed from the fine quality of machine-made tulle; all these had come from Stéphanie's bobbins, and she was having difficulty to continue at her cushion because of her eagerness to explain them. They were French designs, as their charming lines had made me suspect. In the box with the Application were two rolls of Point d'Angleterre, the lace one finds rarely at present. We held the first one, a length of four meters, six inches wide, against the light, and then Stéphanie could sit still no longer; she knew something about this piece, for she had made its first flower in 1911, and not finished its last until the war was half over. She pointed out the spaces where a special needle-worker had introduced almost microscopic open stitches into her leaves and blooms to give them even greater airiness, and showed how almost impossible it would have been to execute these needle-stitches with bobbins; and how difficult is the stitch made with a special crochet-hook required for the raised veins and outlines (brodes) of the petals and leaves, since the hook must catch and attach the thread each time beneath the surface. Finally, a needle-worker, again, as is always the case in Point d'Angleterre, had spun the clear web between the flowers, uniting them all into the finished flounce. Stéphanie pointed to a single detail. "It took me five days to make that tiny bouquet, and the needle-worker one and a half days more to add the open stitches."

Since the snow-covered roads made traveling extremely hazardous, I decided that I could not stop longer, no matter how absorbing the Applications and Points d'Angleterre, or how endearing the personality and contagious the enthusiasm of Stéphanie. I said "Good-by," explaining that I had yet that day to visit the needle-lace school at Zele, twenty kilometers away.

XII

ZELE

XII

ZELE

Stéphanie Visits the Trade Union Lace School

BUT I was not to have to part with Stéphanie. When her Flemish ears gathered from my French that I was starting for Zele and the school founded three years ago, which had been the talk of the region ever since, her eyes fairly spoke her eager desire. Seventy-eight and earning twenty cents a day, and yet consumed by a love for her art (for with her, lace-making is a true art), and a passion to learn more about it! I asked Mme. Coppens if Stéphanie might not come along in the car. In answer she began bustling about, tears in her eyes, to help get her ready, and Stéphanie in her odd little woolen cap could scarcely tie her long black-hooded cape because she was constantly throwing up her hands, and exclaiming, and pressing them together, as she tried to make me understand that in all her seventy-eight years she had only twice ridden in a wagon and never had she dreamed of being in an automobile before she died. What would the neighbors say? We bundled her into the corner of the car and were off, but she could not sit still, leaning forward to exclaim over the beauty of the snow, or a windmill, or the children skating in their sabots, or huddling down to cover her face with her hands in swift shyness if some one had seemed to see her; no spirit was ever so bubbling and gay and eager and timid all at once as Stéphanie's as we rode through the snow toward Zele.

Nor so patient as hers after we arrived; for instead of going to the school, I had to leave her in the car while I went to the house of the director, Dr. Armand Rubbens, unfortunately ill with rheumatism, who is not only the founder of the school but the inspiration of all the unusual accomplishments of the lace-workers of this town, where his father is Burgomaster. After her long wait, Stéphanie's only comment as she looked a little fearfully at the gathering dusk, was: "It is not yet too late to see the school."

Inside, Dr. Rubbens, who since taking his university degree has not been strong enough to follow his profession, and has devoted himself to the 800 lace-workers of his district, explained the organization of the Zele "Trade Union Lace School," founded three years ago and the only one of its kind in Belgium. I felt, as he talked, that he was reproducing in miniature a Henry Ford plant, and when I told him this, he smiled. "I begin to think I should see one of Mr. Ford's factories, for in reading an account of his system in the Paris *Matin* last week, I was astonished at the number of his ideas I had incorporated."

The fifty advanced workers in the atelier (there are 140 apprentices) share the profit of the lace sales in proportion to their wages, and own part of the stock of the union. The best workers of this group make twenty-five centimes an hour, or two and a half francs (fifty cents) a day of eight hours, the highest pay I know of, so far, gained by a lace-maker. The girls may go four hours each week to a school of domestic science, without losing pay; there are illness and pension funds, and other provisions for the health and protection of the members of the school. Dr. Rubbens has seemed to accept every opportunity as a privilege.

I looked over the files and photographs

AT WORK ON DETAILS OF A NEEDLE-POINT SCARF TO BE PRESENTED TO QUEEN ELIZABETH

NEEDLE LACE CLASS-ROOM IN THE TRADE UNION LACE SCHOOL AT ZELE

NEEDLE-POINT ILLUSTRATION FOR THE FABLE OF THE FOX AND THE GRAPES

IN THE ZELE LACE SCHOOL, JOINING DETAILS OF THE NEEDLE-POINT SCARF PRESENTED TO QUEEN ELIZABETH

and records, for even tho Zele is a remote town of but 6,000 inhabitants, this wide-awake director has made it provide for him a better set of records and announcement and advertising cards (some of them in English) than I have seen anywhere else in Belgium. While I was inspecting the books, he opened a chest and spread on the table a finished model from his school—a Needle Point scarf or veil, sown with marguerites and varied by a bewildering succession of open-work stitches, each seemingly more exquisite than the preceding and some of them invented for this particular veil. The needle-workers who had made it had given about 9,000 hours to its flowers and gauze, and it would bring 3,000 francs to the Trade Union treasury.

I felt that I must fetch Stéphanie to see this, but Dr. Rubbens advised hurrying now to the school, where there was something still more beautiful to be seen

—the scarf just completed that will be presented to Queen Elizabeth, and so far the *chef-d'œuvre* of the Zele lace-makers. I told Stéphanie about it on our way through the village.

Once arrived, we went directly to the most advanced class, where Stéphanie might find most to interest her. The young women were at work on Needle Point collars and medallions, a series of tableaux from the legend of the Fox and the Grapes, and she was all eyes and ears as she went eagerly from chair to chair, trying to see what these girls had been taught that she had missed learning, and to add to her lore, if she could. I believe it is only in such a modern school as this that an outsider would have been allowed to examine, as Stéphanie did, the stitches and patterns, for the tradition of the locked door and the carefully guarded secret still prevails in the lace word.

I was impatient to see the school's masterpiece, the royal scarf, and it was now brought from the safe and held before us by three young women, as the directress led us from point to point in the airy mesh spun between its rose garlands and medallions. On either side of the center medallion, the arms of Belgium, were two others, in which human figures symbolized cities the war has made immortal. For Nieuport a fisher-maiden stood on the shore with her basket, and about her the net took up a cockle-shell motif; Poperinghe had the graceful hop-vine as its device; for Furnes there was a dairy-maid with her churn in the midst of blossoming butter flowers; while Ypres was represented by a beautiful Flamande sitting before a lace cushion heaped with bobbins—countless stitches, occupying 12,000 hours, and the entire weight 125 grammes! And yet, at the end, Stéphanie tilted her dear old head and said: "Nevertheless, Madame, for the Queen, I should have made the mesh yet finer."

This Trade Union is in a sense a professional school, since it teaches design, but there is the weak spot in an otherwise remarkable achievement. The designs executed by Dr. Rubbens and the school are often the kind that have led foreign lace-buyers to order through Paris, which could furnish the drawings, rather than direct from Belgium. They lack the lightness and grace that lace designs should unfailingly possess, just the qualities which the Friends of Lace have done so much to encourage and cultivate. If Dr. Rubbens can see his way to follow their suggestions, or to employing a French teacher, there seems no limit to what he may accomplish.

He is now attempting to establish a true needle-lace Normal School, which will offer courses in commerce, English, history, and all the branches necessary to a complete lace education. This will supplement the instruction of the Bruges bobbin-lace Normal, already well under way. He holds that the teaching of the fine needle points is more tedious and difficult than the teaching of the bobbin points, and that it takes more years to become expert in needle laces than in others.

On the way home, Stéphanie asked what she might do for me. "You may pray for me, if you wish, Stéphanie." She was silent a moment. "But, Madame, should I not make a pilgrimage to Lourdes for you? On one of my trips in the wagon, I saw the sea, and for three years after that the sea was every day just before my eyes. And to-day will remain until I die just in front of my eyes. Madame, should I not go to Lourdes for you?"

APPENDIX

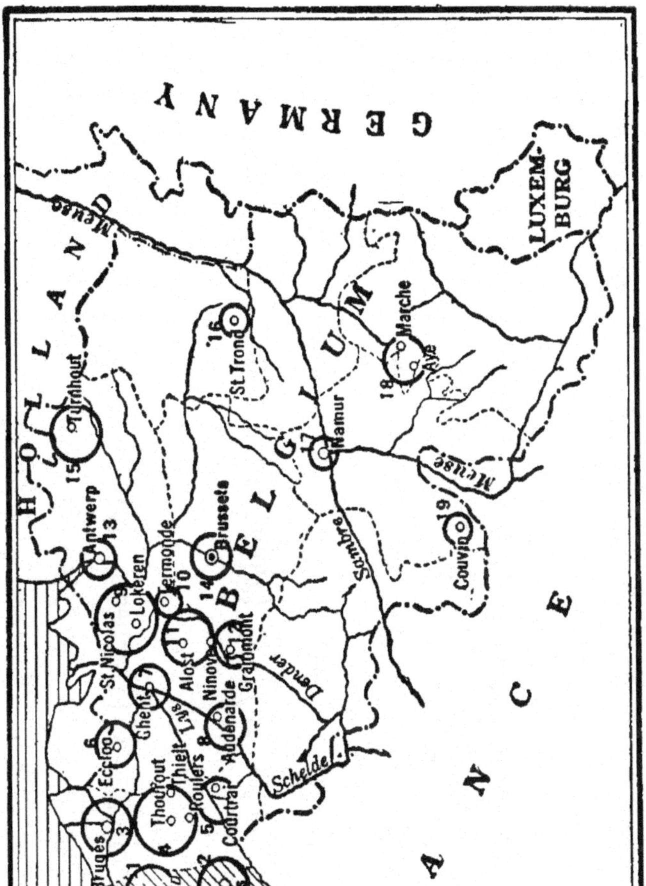
GERMANY
HOLLAND
LUXEMBURG
BELGIUM
FRANCE
NORTH SEA
Meuse
Turnhout
Antwerp
Lokeren
St Nicolas
Termonde
Brussels
St Trond
Namur
Marche
Aye
Couvin
Sambre
Dender
Schelde
Ghent
Alost
Ninove
Grammont
Audenarde
Eecloo
Bruges
Thourout
Thielt
Lys
Roulers
Courtrai
Ypres
Dixmude
DESTROYED AREA
Yser

Map showing important lace areas in 1919, especially prepared for this volume by the Brussels Lace Committee.

The size of the circles indicates the approximate geographical extent of lace-making activity, and has no reference to the quality produced.

The finest varieties are made in the areas indicated by circles 3 (noted for Valenciennes, Bruges, Cluny), 4 (Bruges, Valenciennes, Cluny), 11 (Duchesse, Application, Rosaline), 15 (Maline, Pt. de Paris, Pt. de Lille, Binche).

Second quality, circles 5 (Val., Cluny), 6 (Val., Bruges, Cluny), 7 (Duchesse, Needle Point, Val., Cluny), 9 (Point d'Hollande, Val., Venise, Needle Point, Cluny).

Third quality, circles 8 (Duchesse, Needle Point), 12 (Venise Needle Point, Duchesse, Chantilly), 10 (Bruges, Duchesse, Val., Cluny), 14 (Needle Point, Application), 13 (Cluny, Torchon), 16 (Cluny).

The least important laces are found in regions 17 (Venise, filet), 18 (filet, Torchon), 19 (Point de Paris, Chantilly).

a. Pattern

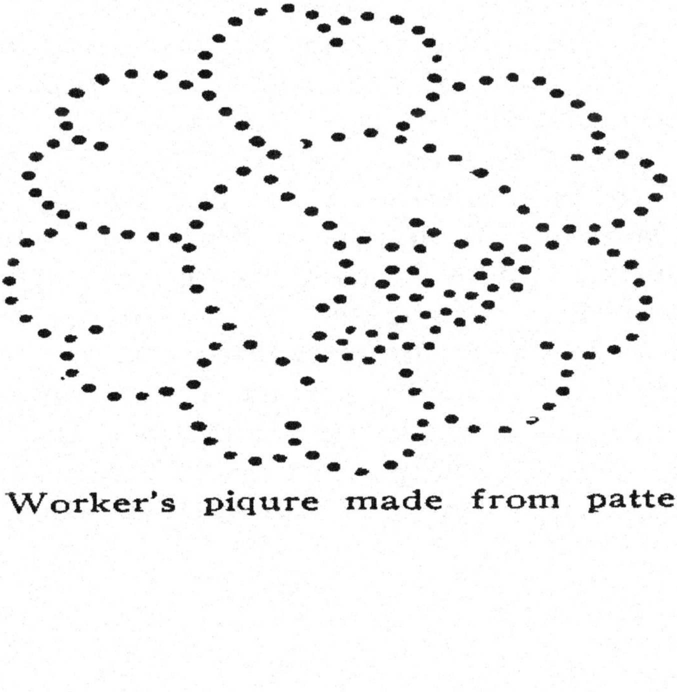

b. Worker's piqure made from pattern

APPENDIX

With Drawings by the Directrice of the Brussels School of Design, Mme. Lucie Paulis

FROM the point of view of technique, all laces are divided into two groups; laces made with the needle, and laces made with bobbins.

I.—Laces Made with the Needle

All needle lace is executed in the same manner. First, the design of the whole is divided into details sufficiently small to allow of their being easily held and turned by the worker. The design of each of these details is reproduced on a special kind of black paper by means of tiny pricked holes that follow all its lines.

The lace worker sews this pattern (or *piqure*) to a piece of double white cloth, which gives it solidity. She is then ready to begin the *tracé* or outlining process. A strand of two or three threads is appliquéd along all the contours of the pattern by means of a very fine needle and very fine thread, which catches the cloth below the black paper, passing and repassing through each of the holes of the pattern, thus holding the

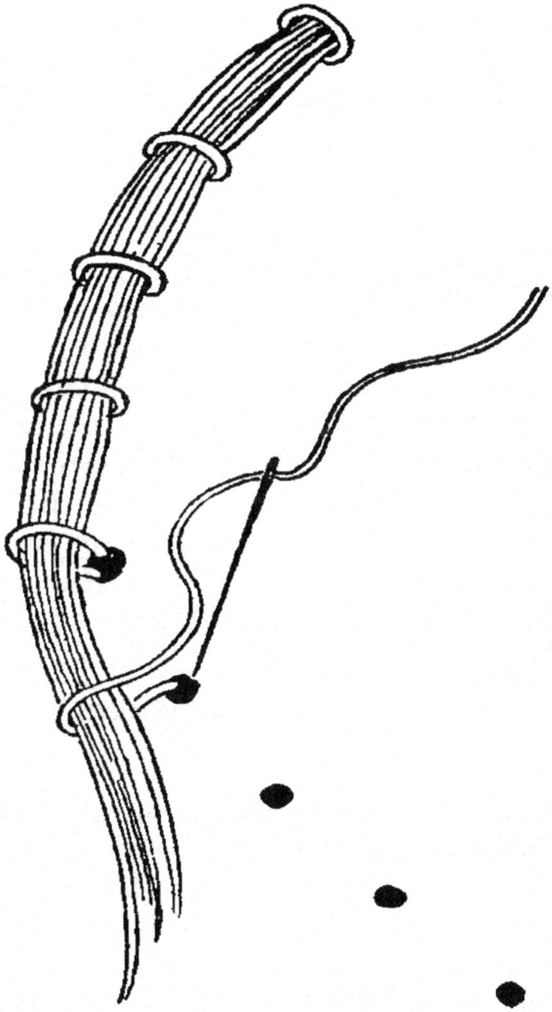

c. The outlining or tracing cord

outlining strand in a sort of embrace. When all the contours of the drawing have been traced, the second part of the work begins, the execution of the points that are to fill in the spaces.

All the points or stitches of needle lace are loops, simple or twisted, formed by a needle carrying a single thread. (The worker holds the needle with the base instead of the point, forward.) The first row of loops is attached to the threads of the outlining strand. Arriving at the extremity of the space she is working, the lacemaker begins a second row of loops running in the opposite direction, attaching each loop to the corresponding loop of the first row. At the end of this row she fastens it to the outlining strand by one or two stitches and starts on the third row, repeating this operation until her space is completely covered.

The *points* or stitches most frequently employed are:

1. The plat (sketch d), or stitch which forms the flat woven parts, which can be more or less tightly drawn, and serves for all the opaque parts of the lace. It is made by simple loops, each row being consolidated by means of a stretched thread as illustrated in the sketch.

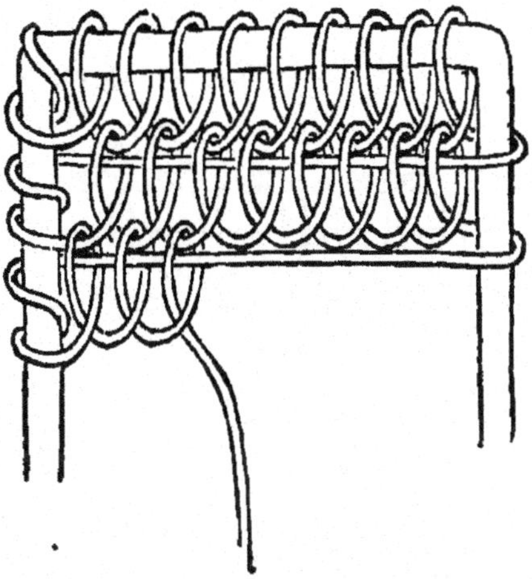

d. Stitch for the *plat* or surface

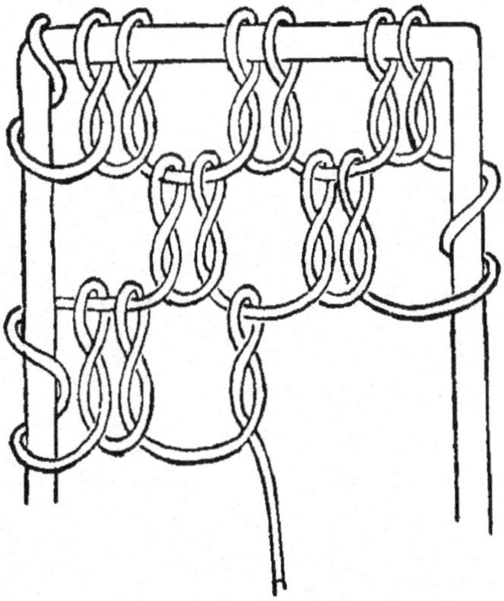

e. Stitch one

The *jours* or open-work stitches. Among the fantasy stitches employed in the jours are:

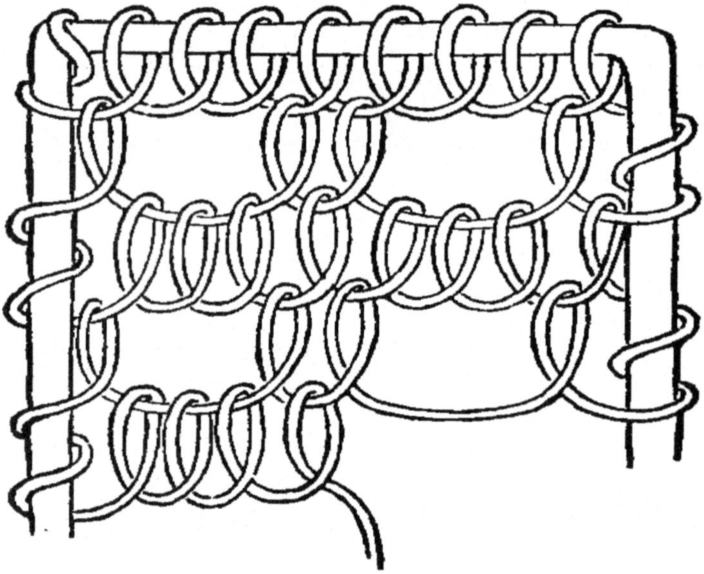

f. Mirror stitch

a. The *point one,* or stitch one, (sketch e.) There exists also a stitch *two,* and stitch *three,* which differ in the number of loops forming the group.

b. The *mirror* stitch (sketch f.) and a kind of *ball* stitch (sketch g.), and lastly the famous extremely transparent *point de gaze,* or gauze stitch (sketch h.), which constitutes the mesh of the popular Brussels lace.

All the surfaces having been covered, the lace is further embellished by the confection of *brodes,* or firm outlining cords around the filled-in

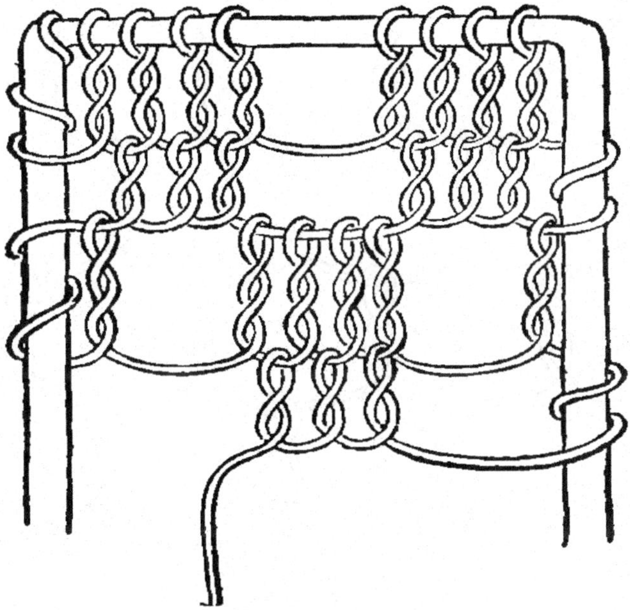

g. Ball stitch

spaces, which produce a more or less striking effect of relief in needle laces. This *brode* (sketch i), is made of a strand of fine or heavier threads, appliquéd as was the original strand outlining the pattern spaces, and then beautifully covered by the buttonhole stitch. When the brode is well made, the buttonhole stitches follow closely, touching side by side.

Many differing little details which help to give

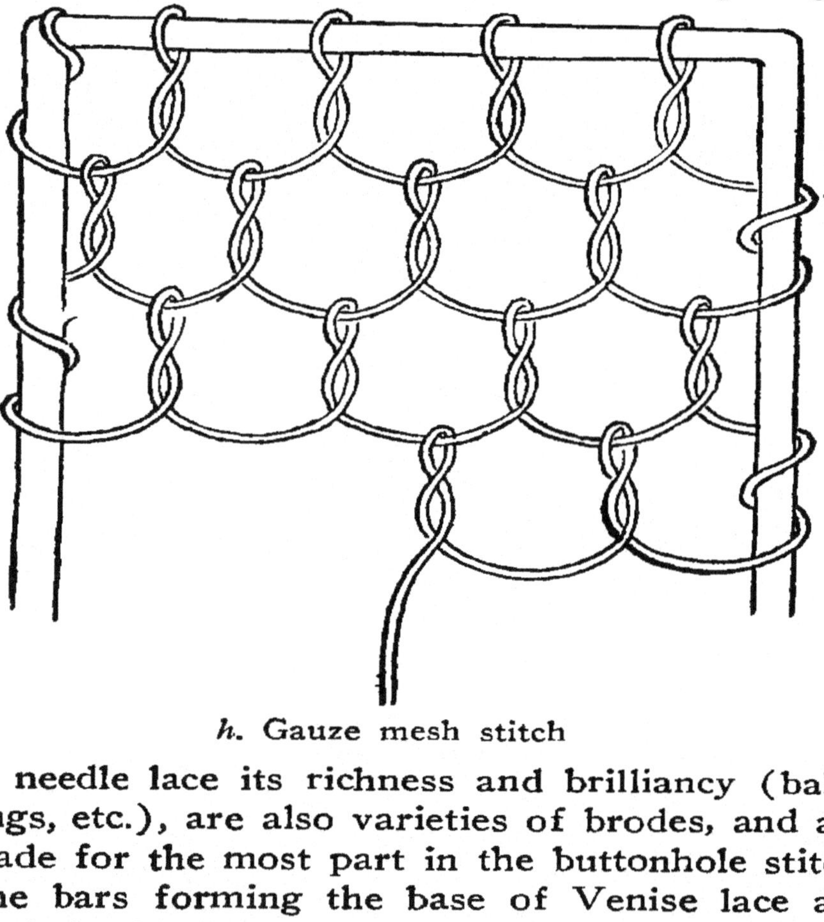

h. Gauze mesh stitch

to needle lace its richness and brilliancy (balls, rings, etc.), are also varieties of brodes, and are made for the most part in the buttonhole stitch. The bars forming the base of Venise lace are made in this way.

The execution of the brodes is the final work

in needle lace. After they are finished, the lace detail is detached from the underlying pattern by cutting the thread between the black paper and supporting cloth, the fine thread which in the beginning attached the outlining strand. There remains only to join the separate details of the pattern by a very fine stitch called the *point invisible*.

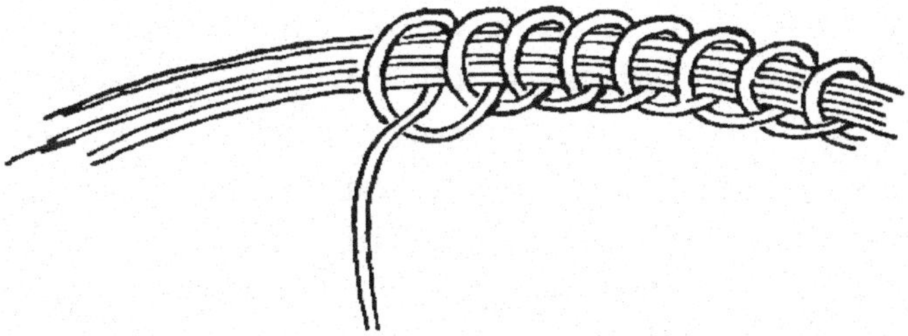

i. Brode, buttonhole stitch

The varieties of needle laces are:

a. Venise (*fond* or base composed of *brides* or bars).

b. Reticella (Venise lace of geometric design and made without brodes or outlining relief cords).

c. Rose Point (Venise with a design of fine branches and tendrils).

d. Brussels Point or Needle Point (very fine lace in which a gauze mesh replaces the bars employed in Venise).

II.—Bobbin Lace

Bobbin laces fall under two groups: (1) Those made with cut threads, and (2) those made with continuous threads.

1. Laces made with cut threads, or of repeated details, are executed on a round cushion, which can be easily turned and they require but a limited number of bobbins (generally not more than two dozen). They may be said to be composed essentially of a braid which grows wider or narrower as it follows all the variations of the pattern, and is interrupted as often as is necessary.

The parts in process of operation are attached to those already finished by veritable running knots made with the aid of a little crochet needle, a tool absolutely indispensable to the making of this kind of lace. The design of the whole is divided into portions so small that they cover only the middle of the cushion. It is necessary to have all around the detail, space for the bobbins, each of which carries a thread about four inches long.

Each fragment is traced on a dark blue paper or *patron* on which the place for the pins is not indicated (sketch k.). The lace-maker pins this blue paper to the middle of her cushion, covering the whole with a piece of dark blue linen which has a hole in the middle large enough to leave free the part of the pattern actually being worked. The

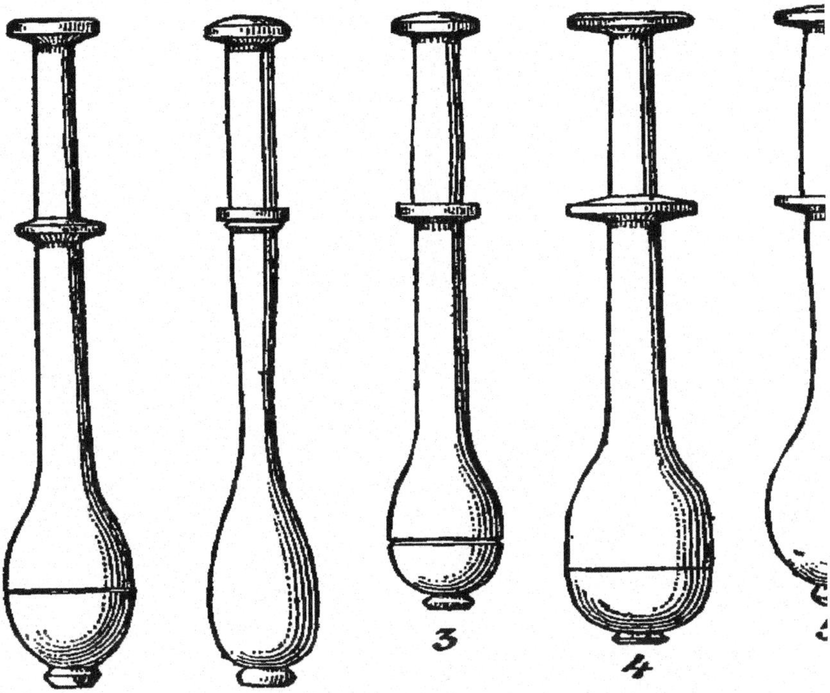

j. Bobbins used in making Belgian laces
1, *2* and *3* Valenciennes
4 and *5* Malines

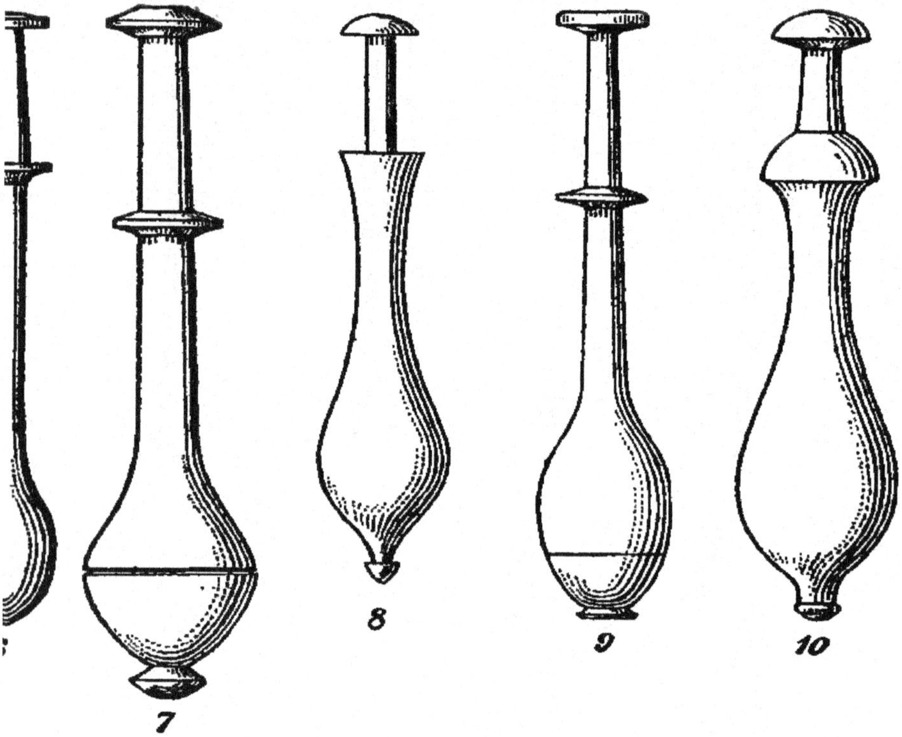

j. Bobbins used in making Belgian laces

6 Malines
7 Point de Paris
8 Application
9 Torchon
10 Duchesse

lace already finished is thus protected. She then places a pin on the spot where she decides to begin, attaching the necessary number of bob-

k. A pattern for bobbin lace, with l. m, n, the braids in which it must be executed

bins and starts to weave as a weaver does, first from right to left, then from left to right, carrying the two bobbins holding the threads forming the woof (*trame*) successively above and below the threads forming the warp (*chaine*). Each time all of the threads of the warp have been

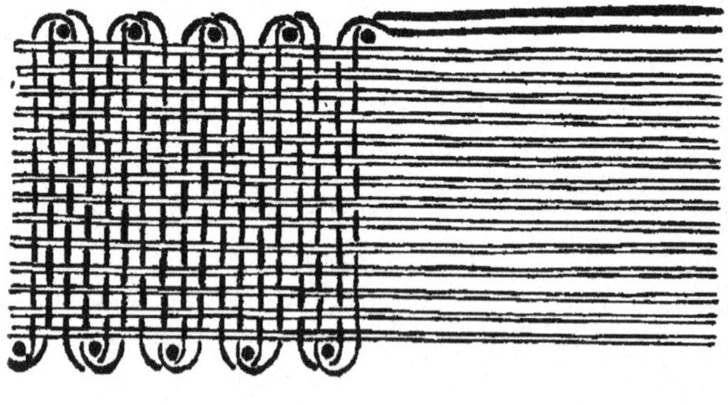

l. A braid which forms the *toile*

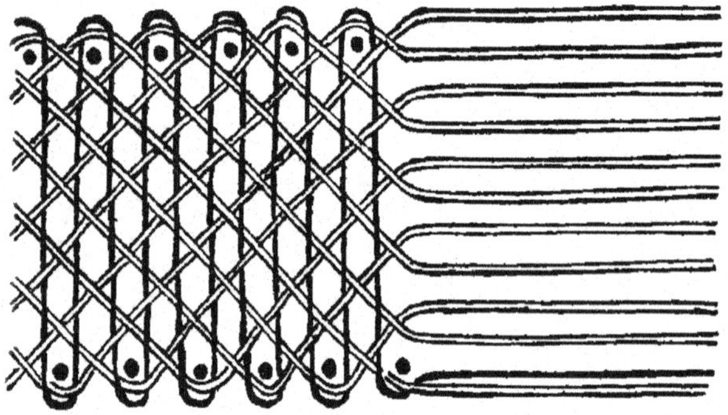

m. A *grillé* braid

n. A braid of 4 threads

crossed by the threads of the woof, she places a pin, and now the two woof threads caught by this pin lead back to the opposite side. She turns her cushion according to the direction of the braid she is executing, so that the threads forming the warp always fall vertically.

The fundamental stitch in these laces and that which forms the greatest part of the braids is the *point de toile,* or *toile* (sketch l.). Certain open stitches are also employed, the most common being the *grille* or half-stitch (sketch m.).

The different varieties of bobbin laces made with cut threads, or in repeated pieces are:

a. Bruges (the flowers are united by brides or bars that are braided with four threads (sketch n.).

b. Duchesse (made only with fine thread, loosely worked and producing a not particularly pleasing result).

c. Rosaline (an imitation with bobbins of Rose Point. Brodes, or raised outlines made with the needle, give it relief).

4. Flanders (in this lace the base of brides or bars is replaced by a net mesh base executed with a needle).

e. Application (the flowers, executed like those of Bruges are sewed upon tulle).

2. Lace made with uncut or continuous

threads. Laces of this group are executed on a stationary cushion. The design, before it can be used by the worker, must pass through the hands of a *piquese,* or interpreter, who prepares what is called the patron or pattern (sketch o), that is to say, determines in advance the places where the pins destined to hold the threads, must be placed (sketch of a piqure, p.). This work of the piquese demands great skill and infinite patience. Upon her interpretation will depend the aspect of the lace, for the worker follows her indications rigidly. This pattern is pricked on a supple and resistant cardboard (in olden times it was made on parchment) and is pinned to the cushion with the selvage of the lace at the left. The worker then attaches to a row of pins placed all across the top of the pattern, the threads which she will need, often many hundreds.

Now she commences her work, braiding, twisting, intercrossing the threads in diverse ways, and placing a pin each time the threads must be held in a position which they can not retain without the aid of a fixt support. When she arrives at the bottom of her pattern, with great care she takes out all the pins, and lifts her work to the top of the pattern, replacing the pins so that the lace will be kept absolutely regular. She then recommences her work of braiding or weaving,

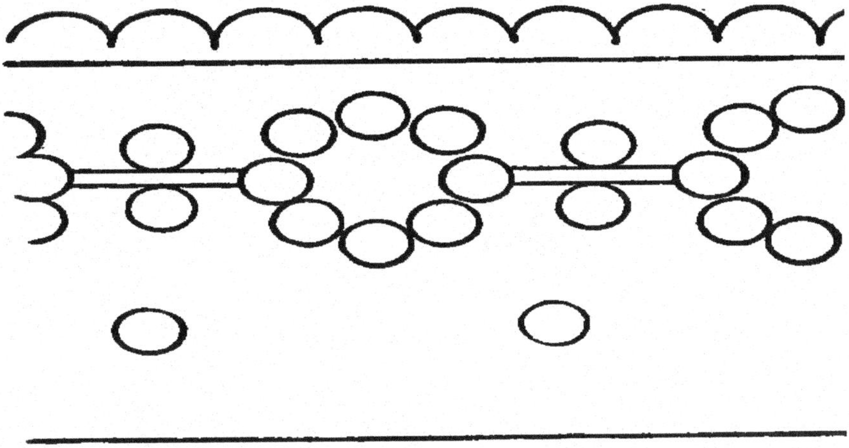

o. Pattern from which piqure is made

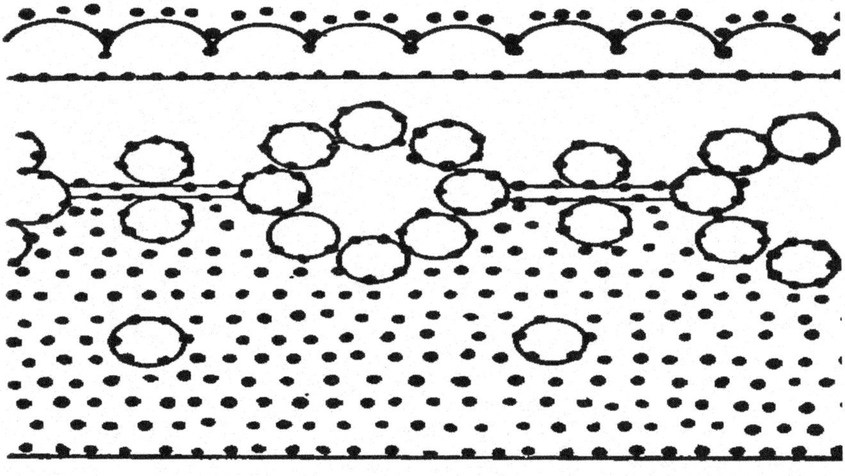

p. Piqure

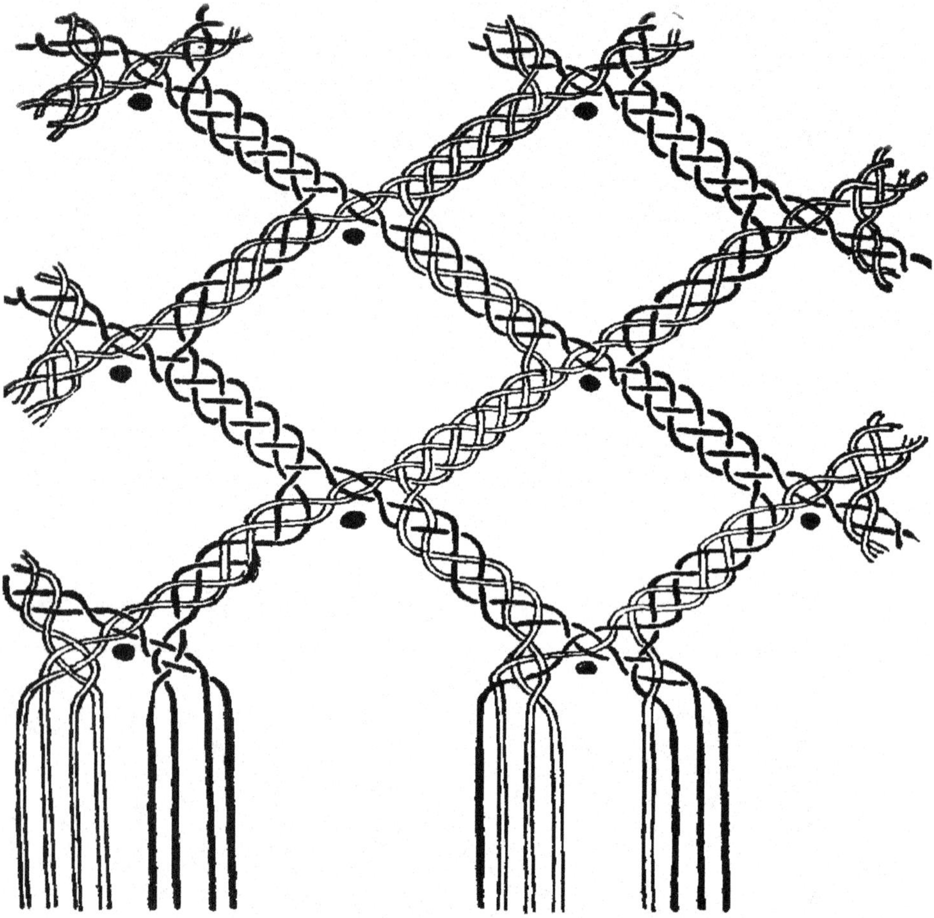

q. Valenciennes mesh

repeating the same operation till the length of lace she must make is finished. The patterns are usually about a foot long.

The bobbin laces made with continuous thread comprise:

a. Cluny and

b. Laces with a mesh base:

1. Valenciennes,
2. Binche,
3. Malines,
4. Point de Paris,
5. Point de Lille,
6. Chantilly.

The varieties in Group *b* may truly be called woven lace, because they contain a veritable tissue in which, tho the threads are combined in such a way as to produce more or less open effects, the opaque parts are woven regularly, that is as linen is woven. The pattern of the mesh of each of these laces is different.

Valenciennes (sketch q.).
Binche (sketch r and s.).
Malines (sketch t.).
Point de Paris (sketch u.).
Point de Lille (sketch v.).

Further, Malines, Chantilly, Point de Lille, and Point de Paris are characterized by the presence of the *bourdon,* or heavy thread, slightly twisted, outlining all the details of the design.

Grammont, or Chantilly lace, is usually made of black silk thread. The mesh is the same as that of Point de Lille. In it the toile is replaced by the grille, which adds greatly to the lightness of the effect.

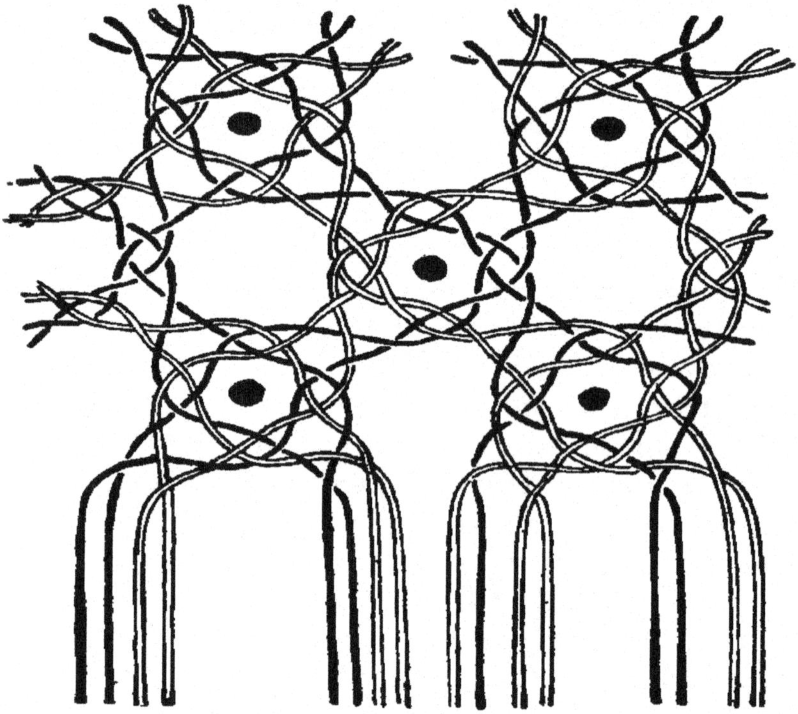

r. Binche mesh

N. B.—To be understood technically, all these laces made with continuous thread should be considered from the point of view of the place they occupy on the cushion of the worker: They are held vertically with the selvage at the left.

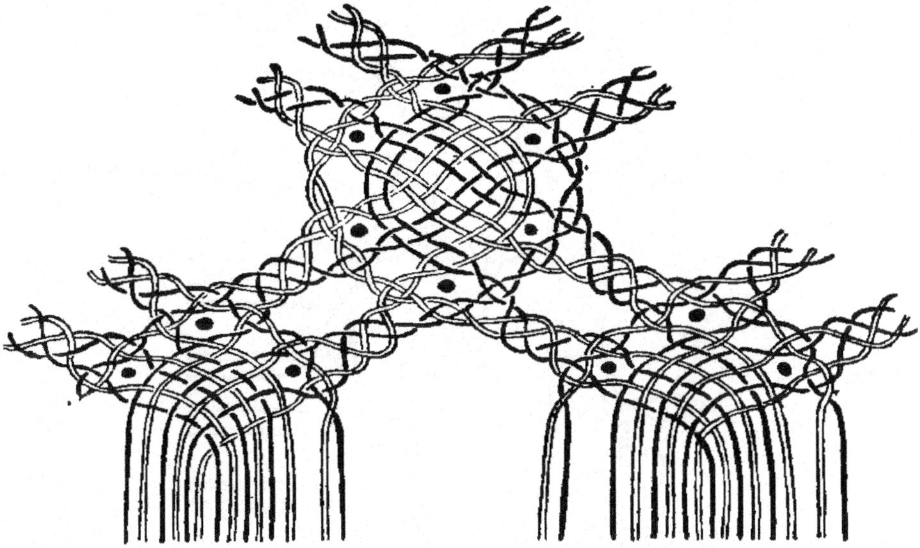

s. Mesh of "snow-ball" pattern, used in Binche

It is necessary to mention with these laces, Torchon, the most common of all, which has little artistic value, and has entered more and more into the domain of the machine. Torchon base (sketch w.).

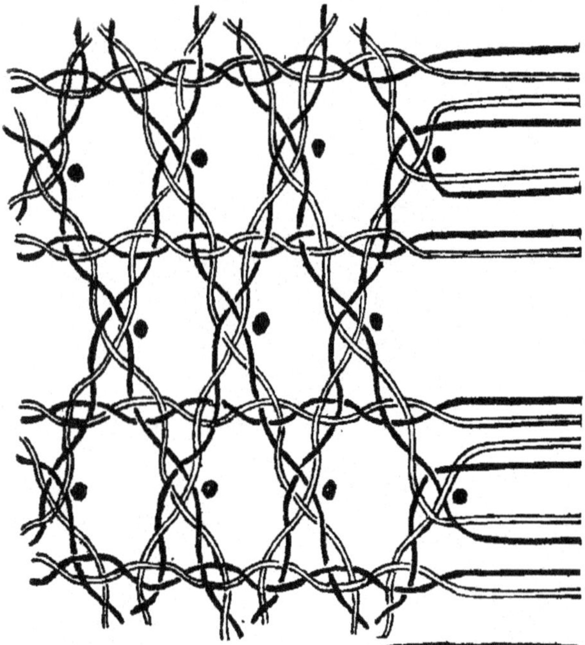

u. Point de Paris mesh

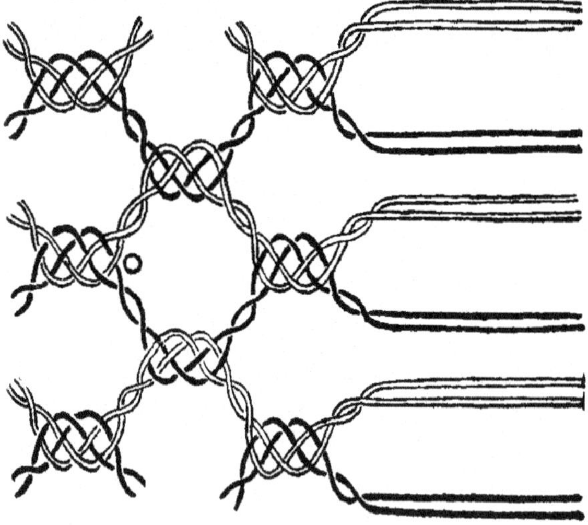

t. Malines mesh

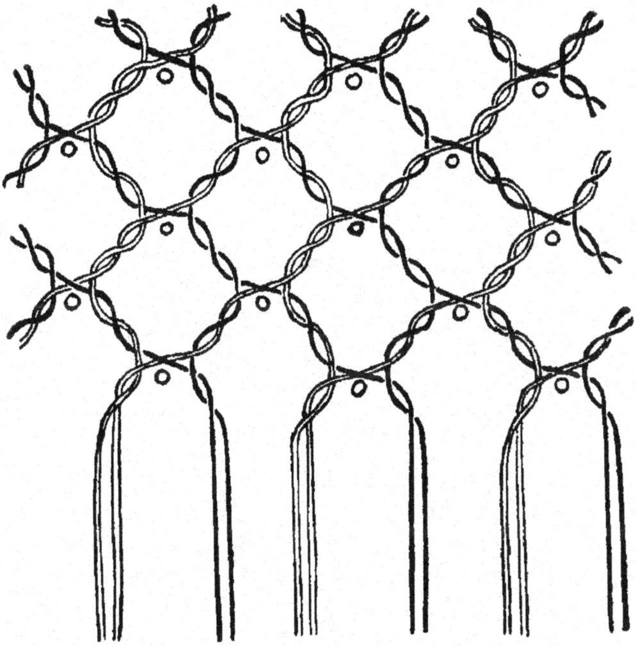

v. Point de Lille mesh

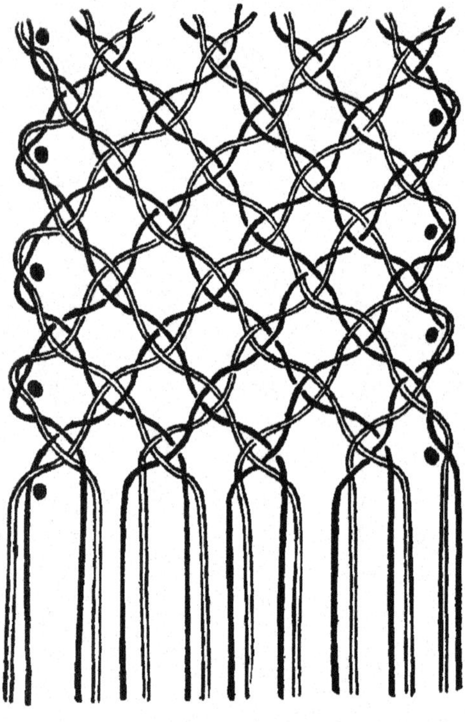

w. Torchon base

Group *A.*—Cluny laces demand great ingenuity in execution. The most simple are made entirely by braiding in such a way as to produce an effect of interlacing (sketch y.). The braids are

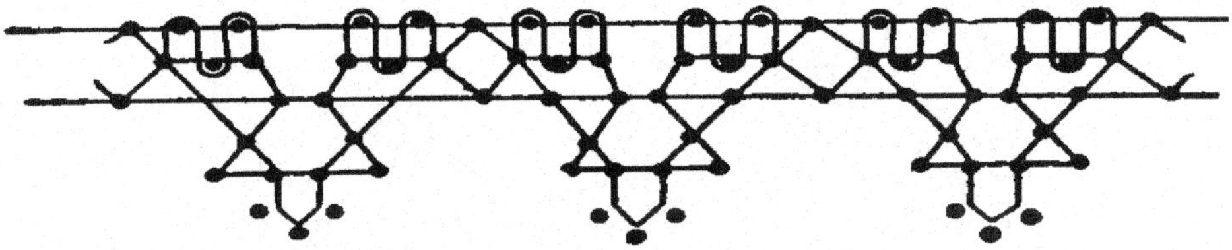

x. Picot

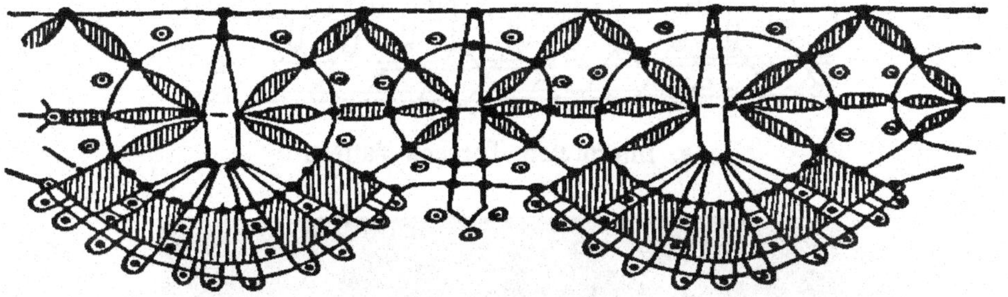

y. Cluny pattern

formed of four threads; when the interlacing is more important they become more complicated. At times the braids group themselves to form the flat surface or toile which later will resolve again into braids. They unite and part, sometimes dividing into strands (brides) of two threads according to the lines of the design. This design should be

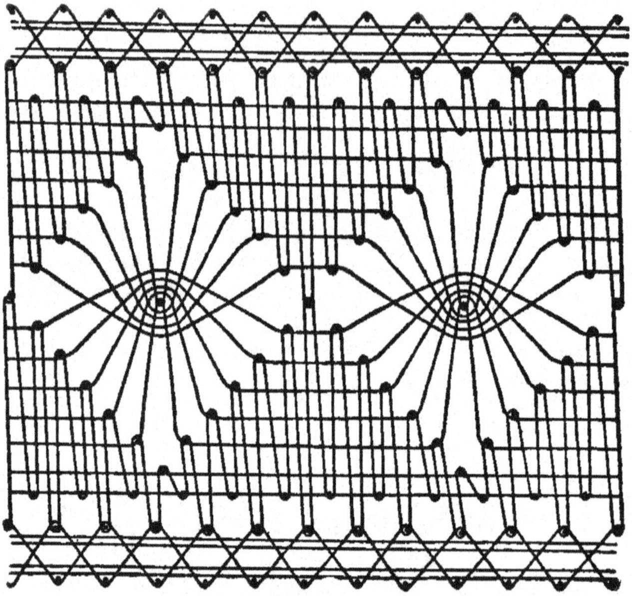

2. Interpreted Torchon pattern

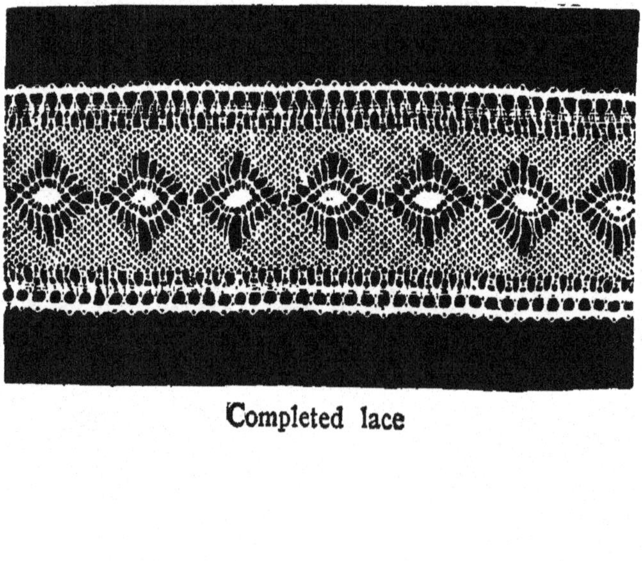

Completed lace

absolutely precise. And since in it the future employment of each thread must be constantly foreseen, it is quite impossible to compose a Cluny lace pattern without a knowledge of the technique of that lace (sketch y).

Sometimes the general name guipure is given to Cluny, as well as to all laces made with continuous thread which have not a mesh base.

INDEX

INDEX

CPSIA information can be obtained at www.ICGtesting.com
Printed in the USA
BVOW06s2249270416

445905BV00022BA/208/P

9 781313 396899